Hindu Gods and Goddesses

A G Mitchell

UBS Publishers' Distributors Ltd.
New Delhi ● Bombay ● Bangalore ● Madras
Calcutta ● Patna ● Kanpur ● London

UBS Publishers' Distributors Ltd.

5 Ansari Road, New Delhi-110 002
Phones : 3273601, 3266646 ✰ *Cable* : ALLBOOKS ✰ *Fax* : (91) 11-327-6593
e-mail: ubspd.del@smy.sprintrpg.ems.vsnl.net.in
Apeejay Chambers, 5 Wallace Street, Mumbai-400 001
Phones : 2046971, 2047700 ✰ *Cable* : UBSIPUB ✰ *Fax* : 2040827
10 First Main Road, Gandhi Nagar, Bangalore-560 009
Phones : 2263901, 2263902, 2253903 ✰ *Cable* : ALLBOOKS ✰ *Fax* : 2263904
6, Sivaganga Road, Nungambakkam, Chennai-600 034
Phone : 8276355 ✰ *Cable* : UBSIPUB ✰ *Fax* : 8270189
8/1-B, Chowringhee Lane, Calcutta-700 016
Phones : 2441821, 2442910, 2449473 ✰ *Cable* : UBSIPUBS ✰ *Fax* : 2450027
5 A, Rajendra Nagar, Patna-800 016
Phones : 652856, 653973, 656170 ✰ *Cable* : UBSPUB ✰ *Fax* : 656169
80, Noronha Road, Cantonment, Kanpur-208 004
Phones : 369124, 362665, 357488 ✰ *Fax* : 315122

First Indian Reprint	1992
Second Indian Reprint	1993
Third Indian Reprint	1993
Fourth Indian Reprint	1994
Fifth Indian Reprint	1994
Sixth Indian Reprint	1995
Seventh Indian Reprint	1996
Eighth Indian Reprint	1996
Ninth Indian Reprint	1997

Cover Design : UBS Art Studio.

Printed at Nutech Photolithographers Shahdara, Delhi-110 095

CONTENTS

Deities are listed by plate number

Hinduism is an all-embracing word for which it is impossible to give a simple definition. One of its meanings covers the religion of India which was introduced by the Aryan settlers and has been modified almost continuously ever since in response to the teaching of other religions (including folk religion), the development of ideas, and the needs of local communities. As a result it is an amalgam of sects, cults, and doctrines which has had a profound effect on Indian culture. In spite of this diversity, there can be few of its aspects which do not rely in some way or another (as do the forms of its deities) on the authority of Indian religious literature particularly the Vedas, Epics and Puranas.

Vedic deities
These belong to the ancient period of Aryan migrations, possibly from the southern steppes of Russia, into north west Pakistan between about 1700 to 700 B.C. The Aryans were culturally akin to similar peoples who were invading Europe at about the same time; the Sanskrit language of their religious texts (Vedas) is related to many European languages, such as Greek and Latin, and some of their deities are also found in Greek mythology (Dyaus, the sky god, i.e. Zeus). It is likely that the Vedic gods who eventually became established in India were the result of the fusion of ideas brought by the invading Aryans and those of indigenous people such as the Dravidians. Although the Aryans were mainly herdsmen they put less emphasis on the propitiation of pastoral deities than on the deification of more fundamental and abstract conceptions and natural phenomena such as the sun (Surya), and fire (Agni). These deities were defined in the Vedas together with meticulous descriptions of the ceremonies that were intended to coerce them into bringing about material benefit in this world for the worshipper. It is evident from the Vedas that deities were, to a certain extent, visualized as having human or animal forms although the degree to which this happened was not the same in all cases. It does not follow that they were worshipped in the form of images, and the question of whether this took place is controversial. This ambiguity is perhaps the strongest evidence against image worship in the Vedic period as it is at variance with the precise descriptions of other aspects of ritual that were given in the texts (see also under Puranic deities below). There remains the possibility, important for its effect on the later development of images, that some of the lower strata of the population worshipped images in human or animal form and that this practice gradually spread upwards to other sections of society. At a much later period, Vedic deities were retrospectively given human form and reproduced as images. The bronze figure of Surya (*pl.1*) is an example of this process.

As a result of the Aryans' further penetration into India and thus greater contact with the local inhabitants, and in response to inevitable forces of development, the old Vedic religion underwent several changes. These chiefly concerned the deities that were worshipped and the forms of ritual. Some deities changed their function, or gained or lost prestige, while the powers of intercession between deity and layman became monopolized by the priests (Brahmans) who alone could perform the necessary sacrifices. This tended to emphasize still more the remoteness of some deities such as Vayu, the Vedic wind-god, and Indra (king of the gods and god of the thunderstorm), and to increase the awesomeness of others like Varuna, guardian of the cosmic order. Consequently, many of the old deities were assigned to minor positions in the pantheon, others were promoted, and new deities were introduced. Parallel with this, the need gradually arose for a more satisfying relationship between the worshipper and the worshipped which became widespread. This need for devotion (*bhakti*) towards a personal god stimulated the desire for images which would make the deity more easily approachable. Their introduction was almost certainly a slow, uneven process and it is likely that images were at first only made of minor deities in the pantheon. It is, perhaps, significant that one of the earliest unambiguous references to images for worship (by Panini, about the 5th century B.C.) is of *yakshas* (tree spirits) and *nagas* (snake gods), and that some of the earliest Indian images of deities (e.g. the stone torso from Parkham, 3rd century B.C.) are probably of *yakshas* rather than of Vedic deities.

Epic deities
Further stimulus to a more personal relationship between gods and men was given by the two great epic poems of Indian literature, the *Ramayana* and the *Mahabharata*, which were written between about 300 B.C. and A.D. 300. Although secular works, the stories they tell not only describe the feats of their heroic characters but refer to the influence that the gods had on their exploits. Thus the stories of the gods were added to and expanded as they were woven into the narratives and, predictably, the heroes themselves succumbed to the assimilative powers of Indian popular religion and became deified. (*see pls.17,18, and 43–45*).

Puranic deities
The further development of Indian society brought about corresponding changes in religious concepts and an increase in the size of the pantheon. This grew by a process of absorption and syncretism, not unlike the Arthurian legends, adopting popular (including female) deities into a sophisticated and well developed assembly or merging several deities into one. Thus the minor Vedic deity Vishnu was identified with Vasudeva and another Epic hero Krishna. It is likely that the ten incarnations (*avataras*) of Vishnu (*see pls.6–18*) that eventually became conventional were attributed to him in a similar way. Later, Krishna himself absorbed a pastoral

flute-playing deity (*pl.20*) and became the subject of many poems and legends. At the same time, an ancient fertility god, Shiva, was promoted to the higher ranks of the pantheon and became an important deity with a variety of forms that gave him a popularity equal to that of Vishnu (*pls.31– 35*). In one aspect of Hinduism, Vishnu and Shiva were visualized as forming a triad with Brahma (*pls.2 and 3*) but, in spite of his ancient prestige, Brahma never received the widespread adoration enjoyed by the other two gods. Beginning about the 4th or 5th century A.D. attempts were made to create some sort of order out of the mass of myths and legends that had evolved round a large number of deities. Eventually these trad- itional tales were incorporated into the Puranas ('Ancient Stories') that formed compendia summing up all that was known about the gods con- tained in the Vedas and Epics, linking the gods by elaborate genealogies, providing religious instructions, and inserting many interpolations. In consequence, much of the appearance of deities that have been made sub- sequently (including those illustrated below) is the result of formalization given to them in the Puranas.

At the same time a further impetus was given to Hindu mythology (and thus a corresponding increase in the number of deities) by the development of Tantrism which emphasized the cult of the female partner (*shakti*) in association with her male deity, often Shiva, (*see pl.34*). From the 15th century onwards a revival of interest in the *bhakti* movement brought about a widespread devotion to the cult of Krishna. Nor have the creative powers of India's religious life declined during recent years but continue with the same energy as they had in the Gupta period (4th–6th century A.D.). The ancient Mother Goddess was born again as Bharat Mata (Mother India) by the efforts of the nineteenth century Bengali novelist Bankim Chandra Chatterjee, and is worshipped in shrines in the form of a map of India. More recently (in 1960) the goddess Santoshi Mata appeared complete with her own mythology and legends in northern India where, conventionally, her help is invoked for personal advancement and material gain. As each new deity was accepted as the legitimate object of worship it attracted a corresponding body of literature. Some of this, and commentaries on existing texts, was written by thinkers who achieved such fame and influence that they (or their devotees) became objects of worship in the form of images (*pls.30 and 49*).

Thus image worship crept almost imperceptibly into Indian religions and was not only finally sanctioned in these scriptures but the images themselves and the rituals for their worship were also described in great detail. One of the results of this process, perhaps more especially the merging of two or more deities, was that some gods were envisaged as holding several attributes (*see pl.47*) or making gestures, *mudras*, (*see pl.11*) that both symbolized their individual powers and differentiated them from other deities. The visual problems that this created for the sculptor when he made images of the gods were solved and conventionalized by showing them with several arms.

Bronze sculpture technique

Here, and in the rest of this introduction, and sometimes in the short description of each caption to the plates, the word bronze is used in its generic sense for metal images that could be made in bronze, brass, or copper. In cases where the type of metal is known (e.g. brass) it is stated in the caption. The technique for making images in all three metals is roughly the same, with only slight variations according to the different casting properties. The present tense is used to describe the technique which is still in use today.

It has been shown above how the form that images took was often governed by their textual descriptions, either forming part of a narrative or given in ritual passages. The latter are of three kinds, of which *dhyanas* describing the visual and spiritual aspects of a deity are the most important. From these, and traditions acquired during his apprenticeship, the sculptor (*sthapati*) knows how a deity should look (how many arms, what kind of jewellery, its hairstyle, posture, etc.) to be suitable for the purpose for which it is intended. The next stage is to decide the proportions of the parts of the image on which its aesthetic qualities will so much depend. Detailed rules for these are laid down in texts on iconography, such as the *Brihat Samhita* which belongs to about the 5th century A.D. but is based on much earlier material. They divide the figure according to the number of 'faces' in its height, similar to systems found in ancient Greece. In the most common system, the length of the face (i.e. one *tala*) was measured eight times for the length of the body, so that the whole figure was nine *talas* in height. The *tala* was subdivided into 12 *angulas* which was then subdivided and so on to give the minute subdivisons needed for the correct proportions for different parts of the body (e.g. the length of the nose equals four and a half *angulas*). Other systems of basic proportions were used (e.g. for the lesser deities, children) such as one *tala* to six for the body giving a seven *tala* image. The texts also include the proportions for the other two dimensions. To convert these proportions into the actual size of an image, its *tala* (or *angula*) must be provided with an exact measurement. This can be taken from anything, but if it is equated with part of the donor's body, such as the joint of one of his fingers, it enables him to integrate himself in some way with the deity of which he is paying to have an image made. The craftsman is now ready to begin work. He uses the lost-wax (*cire-perdue*) method, similar to that known in ancient Greece, to produce hollow or solid cast images. With slight variations the craft is the same all over India. First, for hollow casting, a rough model of the image is made in clay; this is then covered with a layer of wax in which the fine details are worked. At this stage, the wax model is identical with the finished image apart from its material. Next it is covered with a thick layer of clay which is allowed to harden, and the wax is then run out by heating the mould in a low fire. After this, the molten metal is poured into the mould filling the space left by the wax. When the metal has cooled, the clay is removed leaving the metal image in its rough state. Surplus metal is removed, the image cleaned, rough surfaces are polished, and final details added with a graver. According to the texts, the craftsman should, while he is making images, be in a state of spiritual grace. While the degree that this was observed certainly varied there is little doubt that most of the ancient craftsmen looked on image-making as a religious act. Moreover a well-made image brought health and blessings on this earth to the craftsman as well as the donor. Conversely, if it had defects it could bring misfortune; '. . . if it (the image) be noseless then they (the maker and donor) get ill'. In spite of the apparently strict rules for image-making given in the texts, it is at the same time clear from a comparison of images of the same deity that variations arose in their interpretation which provided the wonderful variety that can be seen in Indian metal sculpture.

Eventually deities were visualized as having a specific colour or colours. Whereas this is almost essential for graphic representations, painted images in sculpture also are not unknown. None are illustrated here, but colour is mentioned in a few of the captions to give examples of its use.

Worship

When the image is finished it is removed from the workshop on an auspicious day and, with appropriate ritual (including perhaps singing and dancing), taken to its shrine and there ceremonially installed and consecrated. Its final resting place may be a temple or a domestic shrine. Each is regarded as the house of the god, and the series of religious observances that are performed throughout the day are intended to provide for its well-being such as waking in the morning, bathing, feeding, amusement, and putting to rest at night. Hindu worship (*puja*) is not congregational, in the Christian sense, except in sects which put great emphasis on devotion (*bhakti, see pls. 19 and 30*) where it is specifically encouraged. In the temple the devotee may be present at the fixed ceremonies mentioned above, he may employ a priest to carry out a ritual for him, or summon the god's attention on his own to hear, perhaps, a supplication or receive an offering made as the result of a vow. *Puja*, however, varies considerably in its details depending on the sect, the size of the temple and its location, etc. Domestic worship, for which most of the images shown in this booklet were probably intended, also varies according to individual needs and inclinations. A princely household may employ its own domestic chaplain (*purohita*) while others may invite a Brahman (or a travelling *guru*) to perform ceremonies for special occasions. An orthodox believer could rise early and spend most of the day worshipping a deity of which a properly consecrated image is not merely a symbol but the point at which, at least temporarily, the deity is present. This might include all the daily offices mentioned above, or several other rituals including making offerings of flowers and food, reading the scriptures, and reciting prayers. Alternatively, a busy devotee might restrict himself to a prayer and some breathing exercises morning and evening, and a visit to a large temple perhaps two or three times a year for the most important festivals.

Figure I Hand gestures (*mudras*), hair styles, symbols, etc

b. *Abhaya-mudra*

c. *Kataka-mudra*

a. *Varada-mudra*

e. *Kiritamukuta*

d. *Jatamukuta*

f. *Karandamukuta*

Figure I (*continued*)

g. *Vitarka-mudra*

h. *Anjali-mudra*

i. *Makara*

j. *Kirtimukha*

k. Conch shell (*shanka*)

l. Discus or
wheel (*chakra*)

m. Rosary (*akshamala*)

Figure II Symbols and weapons

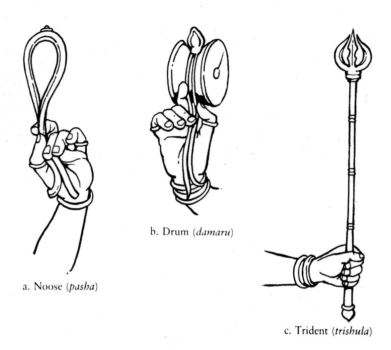

a. Noose (*pasha*)

b. Drum (*damaru*)

c. Trident (*trishula*)

d. *Shakti*

e. Antelope

f. Open lotus (*padma*)

Figure II (*continued*)

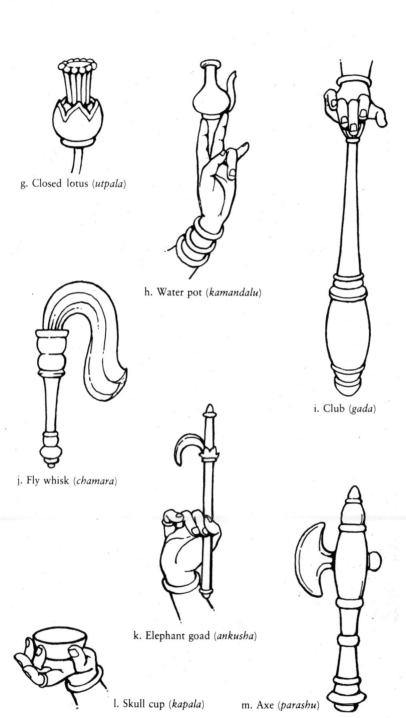

g. Closed lotus (*utpala*)

h. Water pot (*kamandalu*)

i. Club (*gada*)

j. Fly whisk (*chamara*)

k. Elephant goad (*ankusha*)

l. Skull cup (*kapala*)

m. Axe (*parashu*)

Bronzes in India

It is most probable that texts (orally transmitted) preceded image-making in India and that, therefore, images were based on them. But, with Hinduism's tendency to absorb myths from outside sources, it is possible that a two-way process developed particularly from about the 5th century onwards. Disregarding coins, Hindu images from the early centuries A.D. are rare, which may mean that, if they existed at all, they were made of perishable material. Suggestions that they were known at an earlier period should be treated with caution as the famous so-called 'dancing girl' from Mohenjo Daró has not been proved to be an image of a deity. From the examples of religious sculpture that have survived it seems that stone icons preceded bronze, the earliest of which belongs to the first century A.D. A small number can be ascribed to the late Gandhara period (about the 5th century A.D.) and the Gupta (4th–6th centuries A.D.) most of which are Buddha figures. They show a mature technique in interpreting stone sculpture styles which implies much previous experience which has not as yet been accounted for. Slightly later (about 5th–7th centuries A.D.), the bronze Buddha from Sultanganj now in the Birmingham Museum, is a most impressive example of India's art of metal sculpture not only at this period but at any time. By the beginning of the Pala period (A.D. c.750–1160), bronzes began to be made in much larger numbers. Responding to a period of comparative peace and increase of wealth, an expansion of interest in religion brought about a greater demand for bronze images both Buddhist and Hindu. Some of these were probably intended, like the Sultanganj Buddha, to be installed in an institution such as a monastery but the majority were small and therefore likely to be for domestic use. Many of them are of very high quality, and some are inlaid with gold, silver or copper, or set with stones; others carry inscriptions by which they can be dated. Corresponding to this increase in numbers there was a parallel increase in the different types of deity of which bronze images were made. It was as if the gods, lurking in the old texts and hinted at in late Gupta sculpture, suddenly flowered in the form of images for a brief period before it was ended by the Muslims or they were exiled to the south. There, bronze image casting had probably reached its height in technique and aesthetic quality during the Chola period (mid-9th to mid-13th centuries A.D.) when some of India's finest bronzes were produced. They combine a delicate sensitivity in their treatment of details, especially facial features, with a graceful vigour in their posture and assured balance in their proportions. Many of the best examples remain in worship in temples in South India. Excellent bronzes were also made in western India, but those for Jain use are as a rule iconographically less interesting than the Buddhist and Hindu, and their style is rather static and limited in its range of expression. Hindu bronzes continued to be made in the south during the 14th and 15th centuries, some of which are worthy of comparison with the Chola images, but the quality declined as the quantity increased from the late Vijayanagar period onwards (17th–19th centuries).

Most of the bronzes illustrated here belong to the 19th century. Although hardly comparable with the finest of the older examples, they are often well made and show a deep respect for tradition and evident spirituality. Moreover some of those from South India (*e.g. pls.7–16*) represent a clearly defined style which is shared by a large group of bronzes. There can be little doubt that the best of them are worthy successors to the ancient skill of metal image-making in India. Those having a single accession number (*e.g. pl.1*) originally belonged to the collections of the East India Company Museum and were transferred to the Victoria & Albert Museum in 1880 or earlier. They are published here for the first time.

Bibliography

*Banerjea, J. N., *The Development of Hindu Iconography*, Calcutta, 1956.

*Daniélou, A., *Hindu Polytheism*, London, 1964.

Dowson, J., *A Classical Dictionary of Hindu Mythology*, London, 1972.

Gangoly, O. C., *South Indian Bronzes*, Calcutta, 1915.

Hopkins, E. W., *Epic Mythology*, Varanasi, 1968.

Liebert, G., *Iconographic Dictionary of the Indian Religions*, Leiden, 1976.

Mani, Vettam, *Puranic Encyclopaedia*, Delhi, 1975.

†O'Flaherty, W. D., *Hindu Myths*, Harmondsworth, 1978.

Rao, T. A. Gopinatha, *Elements of Hindu Iconography*, (2 vols.), Madras, 1914.

Sastri, H. K., *South-Indian Images of Gods and Goddesses*, Madras, 1916.

*Srinivasan, P. R., *Bronzes of South India* (Bull. of the Madras Gov. Mus., New Series, vol. VIII), Madras, 1963.

*Contains a bibliography
†Contains a bibliography and bibliographical notes

PLATE 1

Surya (Surya Narayana)

Surya is one of the more important deities of the Vedas (the others being Agni, Soma, Indra, and Vayu) and personifies the sun. He thus corresponds to similar deities in many primitive religions outside India where he is regarded as the source of light and warmth, and even of life itself. In Indian mythology he is by extension the source of all knowledge and, as the origin of solar energy, of the laws that govern the universe and human society. In pastoral or agricultural communities his daily progress across the sky, control of the seasons, and power to grant or withhold the ripening of the crops on which the economy was based put him among the highest of the gods. In ancient Indian literature there are described many ways of regarding this deity which are reflected in some of his names, Diakara (daymaker), Grahapati (king of the planets) etc.

According to the descriptions of Surya in later (i.e. non-Vedic) texts reference is often made to his appearance as being 'in northern garb', and this may account for his being shown in north Indian images as wearing long boots reaching to his knees. In south Indian images, however, he is usually shown bare-footed. Whether seated or standing, his main characteristics are the lotuses, held one in each hand at shoulder level. He may also be shown in a chariot (perhaps with only one wheel), that carries him across the sky, drawn by horses the number of which varies but is usually seven.

The figure shown in the illustration is somewhat unconventional; it holds the stems of the usual lotuses in two of the four hands while the others hold the conch and discus. This appearance, except for the transposition of the conch and discus, corresponds to a stone image in a temple in Belur where he also has the seven horses forming the base on which he stands.

1 **Surya** (Surya Narayana), bronze.
South India, probably Mysore; 19th century.
14cm   748 (I.S.)

PLATE 2

Brahma

In the *Rig Veda* the word *brahman* (or *brahma*)* was used to indicate the mysterious power contained in sacred utterances. Later, this was associated with the skill of the priest who spoke the words so that he was described as being *brahman*. In the Upanishads, by a further development, this power was regarded as being universal and forming the elemental matter from which everything (including the gods themselves) originally emerged. Eventually this supreme creative spirit became fully personalized under the name of Brahma.

Since this idea is intimately involved with the origin of the universe it was inevitable that Brahma should become associated with Hindu cosmogony. Many legends grew up, particularly in later texts, surrounding his connexion with the origin and control of the universe. In one of them the supreme soul and self-existent lord created the waters of the earth and deposited in them a seed which became the golden egg, out of which he was born as Brahma. In due course he produced a daughter symbolizing speech, Vach (but also having several other names), by whom he fathered all creatures.

According to other texts, he became a boar who raised the earth from the primaeval waters and thus created the world. In other texts he is described as assuming the appearance of a fish or a tortoise at the beginning of the ages. In much later developments of Hindu mythology these aspects were attributed to Vishnu (*see pl.*6). The image shown opposite has four heads, and four arms holding a rosary (*akshamala*) and water-pot (*kamandalu*) and his other hands in *abhaya* (*left*) and *varada mudras*; he wears a tiger skin as a loin cloth and the sacred cord (*yajnopavita*) over his left shoulder.

*The shortened form of the word for the mystical universal force, *brahma*, ends in a short 'a', as here, but the name of the deity ends in a long 'a' Brahma. No distinction is made between these two words in the text where the deity is referred to throughout as Brahma.

2 **Brahma**, brass; South India (probably Madras), late 18th century. 38.1cm   I.M. 119–1924

PLATE 3

Brahma

In later accounts of the origin of the universe, Brahma's contribution is given a secondary role to that of Vishnu (*see pl.27*), or to Shiva. But in Hindu cosmology the basic cycle, through which the cosmos passes for all eternity, is the *kalpa* or 'day of Brahma', equivalent to 4,320 million years. A night is of equal length, and 360 days and nights of this duration form one year of Brahma's life; this is expected to last 100 years (at present he is regarded as being aged 51 years (*see pl.13*).

In spite of his apparent importance in the earliest myths of the creation of the universe, which was reflected in the prestige attributed to him in the early Buddhist scriptures and in the *Mahabharata*, his worship slowly declined and has not been widespread since about the 6th century A.D. Images of him are still made, however, and many temples include one somewhere in their scheme of sculptural decoration although it is only in extremely rare cases that he occupies the position of the main icon. He is usually portrayed with four heads (originally five, but one was burned off by Shiva's third eye) and, if coloured, he is red or pink. He has four arms and may hold a variety of objects in his hands, including a book (the Vedas), a sceptre, a lustration spoon or ladle, a rosary, a bow or a water jug. He is usually, but not always, shown as being a venerable, bearded man. His vehicle is the goose (*hamsa*), symbol of knowledge. In the illustration opposite his symbols are unclear, due to the small size of the image, but his upper hands seem to be holding books.

3 **Brahma**, brass; South India, 19th century.
4.8cm   I.M. 100–1924

PLATE 4

Sarasvati

The cult of the mother goddess has a long history in India, but the emphasis that has been put on it has varied from time to time. In pre-history it seems to have been linked with similar cults associated with fertility rites that were practised further west as in Mesopotamia. Thus, terra cotta figures of what were almost certainly mother goddesses have been found in Indus valley sites that are probably as early as 2500–2000 B.C., and these continued to be made until well into historical times. Some of the early ones were crude, but those from Harappa (about 2000 B.C.) were well made with emphasis on feminine characteristics having wide hips, narrow waist and sometimes large breasts. Despite the difficulty of ascertaining their function, it is probable that they had some connexion with fertility and that they symbolized for their worshippers the creative principle which governed their agricultural economy. Although, perhaps, less importance was attached to the worship of female deities during the Vedic period (about 1500–1300 B.C.), the idea of the Mother Goddess did not die out entirely but was kept alive at popular level by the worship of female tree spirits (*yakshis*) and at the sophisticated religious level by the personification of abstract ideas such as Aditi (primordial originator), Prithivi (mother earth), and deities representing abundance and nourishment such as Sarasvati. Her origins are obscure, but it is possible that she once had something to do with the river Sarasvati in Rajasthan or with water in some other way. At all events, she seems to have been associated with the creative properties that water has for seeds and vegetation.

As for the evolution of the cult of the mother goddess, this eventually had a profound effect on the course of Hinduism and led to the concept of Devi and her offshoots (*see pl.8*), the development of *shaktis* (*see pls.42 and 46*), and the effects of Tantrism (*see pl.48*).

4 **Sarasvati**, bronze. South India (Madras); 19th century.
8.2cm   I.M. 95–1924

PLATE 5

Sarasvati

As well as Sarasvati's underlying association with agriculture, mentioned in the caption to the last plate, she is also connected with a quite different activity.

The deification of speech at the time when the Vedas were being brought together is evidence of the high regard in which the spiritual power of the spoken word was held. This concept was later developed as part of the ritual sacrifices carried out by Brahmans and further expanded to include the magical power of words alone (see pl.42). By a simple logical extension the sacred quality of words and speech was applied to texts and thus to learning. Sarasvati, in addition to being the active power of Brahma, eventually became, as a result of the development in this chain of ideas, the goddess of wisdom and learning, eloquence and the patron deity of music and the arts. Some of her names reflect these aspects of her activities; others are related to her fecundity, or her association with Brahma, which gives her the name Brahmi as an alternative to the one in the heading, the origins of which are obscure.

According to textual descriptions, when painted, she should be white in colour. She may have two arms (as in pl.4), or four as in the illustration opposite, where she holds in her two right hands a lotus bud and a rosary, and in her two left hands a book and a stick of sugar cane. The symbolism of all these (and others that she may hold, including an arrow, bow, mace, discus, conch shell, bell and plough) cannot be dealt with here, but the book, with its connexions with speech, words and learning, and the *vina* (a plucked string instrument) shown in the previous plate are too obvious to need any explanation. In other forms this deity may have a greater number of arms and heads, such as an example from Mysore representing the patron goddess of the 64 sciences that has five heads and ten arms.

5 **Sarasvati**, bronze. South India (Madras); 19th century.
8.5cm I.M. 97–1924

PLATE 6

Vishnu

The career of Vishnu is a striking example of the way in which the changing demands of religious life in India brought about changes in the status of deities or the qualities that they represented. Although a Vishnu is mentioned in the *Rig Veda* he was not at that time a major deity but one who seems to have been venerated for taking three large strides which had great cosmic significance (*see pl.15*). Later he became loosely associated with the sun but did not develop into a solar deity and, eventually, in the *Mahabharata* and the Puranas, he acquired the prestige that he has never lost. Ultimately the qualities with which he became particularly invested were those of permanence, continuity and preservation (in contrast with those of Shiva, *see pls.31 and 35*).

During the course of his development, Vishnu acquired the characteristics of several deities in addition to his own, including a number of popular (in the sense of folk) deities who were absorbed into the Vishnu cult in the form of his incarnations. In the *Mahabharata* he became identified with Krishna in his more martial aspects but these were subsequently replaced by qualities of romantic love, (*see pls.20 and 23*). Vishnu also took on the attributes of several animal deities such as the tortoise, boar, and fish. It is likely that these developments took place slowly and were the result of the absorption of cults that prevailed in different areas of India. Eventually these diverse elements became reduced and systematized into a group of 22 or 39 Vishnu incarnations including those already mentioned. Some of the more common ones were used, with others not in the larger groups, to form a smaller group of ten incarnations (*avataras*). The composition of this group varies but one that is often found comprises, (i) The Fish (Matsya, *pl.11*), (ii) The Tortoise (Kurma, *pl.12*), (iii) The Boar (Varaha, *pl.13*), (iv) The Man lion (Narasimha, *pl.14*), (v) The Dwarf (Vamana, *pl.15*), (vi) Parashurama, *pl.16*, (vii) Rama, *pl.17*, (viii) Balarama, *pl.25*, (ix) Buddha, and (x) Kalkin, *pl.26*.

6 **Vishnu**, copper. South India; 19th century.
32.2cm I.M. 37–1936

PLATE 7

Vishnu *Bhogasthanakamurti*

It is not surprising that the appearance of many images illustrates an incident belonging to the mythology relating to the deity (*see pls.14 and 35*). However, in later texts, such as the Puranas, their appearance was also subjected to classification according to several other criteria. Images of Vishnu were grouped according to whether they were regarded as belonging to the highest (Para), emanating (Vyuha), incarnating (Vibhava), inner controller (Antaryamin), or 'very body of the god' (Arca), form of the deity. These were further subdivided according to the results that were hoped for from the worship of the image (e.g. *bhoga*, attaining wealth and prosperity), its posture (e.g. *sthanaka*, standing) or the composition of the group of deities in which the main image was placed. The shortened conventionalized name of the image shown in this plate merely gives the information that it is a standing image (*murti*, i.e. image) suitable for worship in order to acquire wealth and prosperity. It should be possible to classify all images in this way, but texts dealing with iconography are not consistent and variations are found between the practice adopted in north and south India and between Vaishnavite and Shaivite sects.

In the illustration opposite (*and in pls. 6 and 8; see also fig. 1*) Vishnu is shown holding two of his most characteristic symbols, the wheel (*chakra*) and conch shell (*shanka*). Symbolism forms an important part of Indian iconography where it is used as a form of shorthand to convey some of the personal traits of the deity. The wheel is a particularly potent symbol in Indian mythology and, briefly, represents the Universal Mind and the powers of creation and destruction that form the revolving universe as well as much else besides. The conch is associated with the origin of existence through its spiral form and its connexion with water and (when blown) sound. The club (*gada*), which he also holds, symbolizes authority, or the power of knowledge as the essence of life. As well as the symbolism of objects, hand gestures (*mudras*) are also used either alone or in combination with objects and for the same reason. Here, the open upraised palm is in *abhaya mudra* expressing reassurance.

7 **Vishnu** *Bhogasthanakamurti*, bronze. South India; 19th century. 60cm I.M. 37–1937

PLATE 8

Vishnu, with Shridevi and Bhudevi

Vishnu stands with the wheel (*chakra*) in his upper right hand and a conch shell (*shankha*) in his left, and with his lower right hand in charity (*varada*) gesture, and the left in *katyavalambita* gesture which seems to be of only aesthetic significance. Shridevi is conventionally shown standing on the right of Vishnu, holding in her left hand a pink lotus (*padma*) with its petals open revealing the pericarp; she also often wears a horizontal breast band (*kucha-bandha*). Bhudevi holds in her right hand a blue lotus (*utpala*) which is sometimes differentiated from the pink by having all its petals closed; she does not, as a rule, wear a breast band.

As Hinduism developed, the status of female deities slowly changed from that of mother, sister, or daughter to the representation of the single abstract idea of the sole principle of creative energy. Later, this principle was envisaged as being the active power of the impersonal absolute (Brahman), who was too remote to undertake executive responsibilities and therefore not able to respond to prayers. Eventually this active power was personified in the form of the goddess Devi who could not only respond but also satisfy the worshippers' desire for someone to whom devotion (*bhakti*) could be directed. Further religious developments resulted (by about the 5th century A.D.) in Devi manifesting herself in many different forms as the active power of male deities or as deified symbols of abstract ideas associated with them such as Triple-knowledge (Trayi-vidya), Fierce (Chandi), and Revered (Arya). In the group opposite, Shridevi represents Wealth (another of her names is Lakshmi, *see pl.9*), and Bhudevi (also called Prithivi) the Earth. Eventually this active principle of male deities was formalized as their *shakti* which enabled the pantheon conveniently to be extended and gave the worshipper the choice of approaching the deity directly, indirectly through his *shakti*, or of invoking the *shakti* herself.

8 **Vishnu**, with **Shridevi** on his right and **Bhudevi** on his left; bronze. South India; 19th century.
21cm   I.M. 14–1909

PLATE 9

Lakshmi-Narayana

The word Narayana in the title is an epithet of Vishnu having several meanings ('abode of man', 'moving on the waters', etc.). He is seen here seated with Lakshmi (*see pl.8*) on his left knee. The absence of Lakshmi's breast-band is an example of the freedom and flexibility with which the rules governing the representation of Indian images are observed. Other examples will be found in these pages. Students of Indian iconography will be aware that, in spite of authoritative descriptions of deities given in the sacred texts, many exceptions can be found which account for the variety of representations of the same deity particularly those made for the less sophisticated worshippers.

As well as Lakshmi's association with wealth mentioned in the previous caption, she also acquired a connexion with beauty and, under both aspects, became one of the most popular of Hindu female deities. It is likely that, because of the underlying human desire for wealth and beauty, she absorbed a large number of folk elements during her evolution into a widely accepted member of the pantheon. Some of these may be identified in the qualities attributed to her as Vishnu's wife in several of his incarnations. As Sita (wife of Rama, *see pl.17*) she was said to have been born from a furrow. This has obvious links with agriculture, and its imagery is immediately apparent when it is associated with the working of the Indian plough. This symbolism is again emphasised when she was called Earth (Dharani) as the wife of Vishnu when he was Rama-with-the-Axe (*see pl.16*).

Lakshmi may have four arms when worshipped on her own but is usually shown with two when with Vishnu. She may hold a lotus in her hand and this, in turn, suggests wealth in the form of water which can be so precious in India's climate. Lakshmi-Narayana are conventionally grouped, as they are opposite, with Vishnu supporting Lakshmi with one of his left arms and Lakshmi having her right arm round his shoulders. Two of Vishnu's hands hold the conch-shell (*shanka*) and wheel (*chakra*), and another hand is in *vitarka mudra*.

9 **Lakshmi–Narayana**, bronze, South India; 19th century. 13cm   520 (I.S.)

PLATE 10

Lakshmi-Narayana on Garuda

The two main figures have been described in the caption to the previous plate. They are shown again here to illustrate a slightly different, but very common, context in which images are worshipped. Mention has been made, above, to the tendency in Indian art that resulted from religious requirements in which deities were shown in groups. Some of these were a simple triad, as shown in plate 8, while others consisted of several figures all of which were related to each other through the main figure in some way. The compositional problems which this produced were sometimes solved, as here, by enclosing the group by means of a unit of design that surrounded all or some of the figures. This unit is intended to represent an arch of rays (*prabhatorana*) that springs from the top of two columns at about shoulder level. This is a development of the aureole (*prabhavali*) of light rays that was thought to emanate from all divine beings which, with the halo surrounding the head (*shirashchakra*), was sometimes shown on images from about the 2nd–4th centuries A.D. onwards. Both were perhaps copied from late Greek art and, amongst other visual advantages, helped to relate images carved in high relief with their background. Some were plain, but others were treated decoratively especially during the Pala-Sena period (mid 8th–13th centuries A.D.). During this time the arch was developed often having a *makara* (mythical reptile) at the top of each supporting column and the head of a *kirtimukha* (mythical animal) in the centre at the top, both of which can be seen in the illustration opposite. The leaf motifs behind Vishnu's head are a highly decorative form of the halo.

Both aureole and arch also help to relate the image to the base (*pitha* i.e. seat or throne) to which they are often attached by pegs or slots. Being thus loose, they frequently become detached and images are often found without them. Supporting the main deities, completing the group and illustrating an additional element of Vishnu's mythology is a figure of *Garuda* (*see pl.29*). As well as the simple grouping shown here, others making use of a larger number of figures are also found.

10 **Lakshmi-Narayana** supported by **Garuda**, bronze.
South India; 19th century.
19.6cm   656 (I.S.)

PLATE 11

Matsya

The way in which it is likely that Indian deities absorbed folk elements that eventually became manifestations of that deity has been mentioned above (*pls.6 and 9 and p.vi*), and is also referred to below (*pls.16,34 and 40*). Almost certainly the best examples of this tendency are the ten incarnations (*avataras*) of Vishnu listed in the caption to plate 6. They also partly correspond to the aspect of Vishnu in his role of a creator (*see pl.12*), since they represent the forms that Vishnu takes at the beginning of each *kalpa* (*see pl.13*) in order to appear in the world and become its saviour. The obvious associations between fish and water, linking them with the primaeval waters of creation in Indian mythology (*see pls.2 and 27*), help to give particular emphasis to this aspect of Vishnu as a creator.

There are several versions in the Puranas of the way in which Vishnu assumed the aspect of a fish. One of them describes him as turning himself into a fish so as to tow a ship in which Manu (the Seventh Law-Giver) had taken refuge from a devastating flood. The same story is found in the *Mahabharata*, where the fish is described as having a horn, and in the *Bhagavata Purana* it is further elaborated by the addition of a fight between Matsya and the demon Hayagriva ("Horse-headed") who had stolen the Vedas while Brahma was asleep. Vishnu eventually took on a horse-headed form in the same way that he took on a boar's head after defeating a boar demon (*see pl.13*). The image shown here holds a wheel in its upper right hand and a conch shell in its upper left, and has its lower right hand in *abhaya mudra* and its lower left in *varada mudra*. With only the lower part of the deity in the form of a fish, it closely combines both aspects of Vishnu (main form and *avatara*) and retains the essentially personal element that existed between deity and worshipper in later forms of Indian religions. *Avataras* shown in this way are at least as old as the Pala period in N E India where an example is found on a large panel that may have belonged to a series showing all the ten *avataras* (*dashavataras*) decorating a temple. They seldom formed the main temple icon although this does not rule out the possibility that they could be worshipped individually.

11 **Matsya**, the first incarnation of Vishnu as his fish *avatara*; bronze. South India (probably Madras); 19th century.
15.3cm   553 (I.S.)

PLATE 12

Kurma

This image illustrates the myth in which the gods (sometimes helped by demons) set out to obtain ambrosia (*amrita*) by churning the ocean of milk. They did this by using mount Mandara as a churning rod which they rotated by winding the serpent Ananta (*see pl.27*) round it and pulling first one way and then the other. In the beginning, their attempts failed and, dispirited, they were about to give up when Vishnu encouraged them to continue. He turned himself into a tortoise to act as a pivot for the rod-mountain and this time they were successful.

As well as ambrosia, the churning brought to the surface the other 13 objects that had been lost in the deluge (*see pl.11*) which were, Dhanvantari (the physician of the gods who carried the pot which held the ambrosia), Lakshmi (Vishnu's consort, *see pl.9*), Sura (the goddess of wine), Chandra (the moon), *apsarases* (celestial nymphs), Kaustubha (the precious gem for Vishnu's body), Uchchaihshravas (the divine horse, swift as thought), Parijata (the wish-granting coral tree), Surabhi (the cow that grants all desires), Airavata (the four-tusked elephant), Panchajanya (conch shell), and Sharnga (the invincible bow). Lastly, after more churning, the power of ambrosia was almost neutralized by the appearance of its opposite *halahala* (poison) which for a moment enveloped the universe. But Shiva first held it in his throat (thus giving him one of his names, Blue-throated) and then swallowed it to save all mankind.

Although this is not primarily a creation myth it demonstrates the idea of creation and destruction which is mentioned several times in the pages of this booklet. Briefly, it envisages all parts of the cosmos, from the largest to the smallest unit, as belonging to a cyclical process in which creation and destruction, birth and death, follow each other in eternal rotation. By extension (e.g. the *kalpa*, *see pl.13* and the symbolism of the wheel) these two elements are regarded as being different aspects of the same thing. Although it is thus unwise to try and fit deities wholly into the category of creator or destroyer, Vishnu is more often regarded as belonging to the former and Shiva to the latter.

12 **Kurma**, the second incarnation of Vishnu as his tortoise *avatara*; bronze. South India (probably Madras); 19th century.
15cm   554 (I.S.)

PLATE 13

Varaha

The basic cycle of Hindu cosmology, the 'day of Brahma' (*kalpa*), *see pl.3*, is further sub-divided into other units including four *yugas* that are similar to the Hellenistic four ages and, like them, manifest a steady decline from supreme virtue. We are at present in the last (*Kali-*) *yuga* which is a period of social decay forming part of the 28th *mahayuga* in the 7th *manvantara* of a *Varaha-kalpa*. The reasons for its being given this name are similar to those mentioned in the caption to plate 11 relating to the beginning of other *kalpas*. At the beginning of each *kalpa*, Brahma emerges again from his cosmic sleep out of a lotus growing from Vishnu's navel. After that had happened at the start of the present *kalpa* Vishnu turned himself into a boar (*varaha*) and descended to the bottom of the ocean to rescue the earth which had been abducted and hidden there by a demon. He then brought it to the surface and made it ready to support life by modelling the mountains and shaping the continents. In this way the world was brought into being again to begin another *kalpa* cycle through the intervention of Vishnu. In other words it is a creation myth, perhaps belonging to non-Hindu mythology, that has been incorporated into the Vishnu legend in the form of an *avatara*. The story, which is found in the *Vishnu-Purana*, is probably late but it is the one usually regarded as accounting for the appearance of this *avatara*. There are also others in the ancient texts that associate Vishnu with a boar. One of them is a good example of Vishnu's capacity for adopting the form of his enemies as it describes the way in which he conquers a demon boar who guarded fabulous wealth.

There are roughly two main groups of *varaha avatara* images – those entirely in animal form and those having a boar's head on a human body, similar to the one in the illustration. The latter seems to be the earlier of the two as it includes an example that probably belongs to the 2nd century A.D.

13 **Varaha**, the third incarnation of Vishnu as his boar *avatara*; bronze. South India (probably Madras); 19th century.
15.3cm   556 (I.S.)

PLATE 14

Narasimha

The images of *avataras* illustrated in plates 11–13 have been in the form of part man and part animal. This treatment evolved as a result of the necessity to make the meaning of the icon clear and illustrate more than one aspect of the image such as conveying the idea that it was both a tortoise, for example, and an incarnation of Vishnu. The appearance of the figure shown in the plate opposite, however, springs from its name (*nara* i.e. man, *simha* i.e. lion) which comes from textual descriptions that refer to a deity who is half man, half lion. Vishnu assumed this appearance in order to overcome a demon king who could be slain neither by man nor beast, inside or outside a palace, by day or night. Adopting the form of a lion-headed man, Vishnu approached the palace at dusk and hid in a pillar at the entrance out of which he sprang and killed the demon king Hiran-yakashipu. Some sculptures show this incident taking place inside a pillar, and others show Narasimha with Hiranyakashipu on his lap tearing out his entrails. There are other forms which, as a consequence of the tendency in Hinduism for deities to develop different forms which is referred to several times in these pages, show a synthesis of aspects of Vishnu and Narasimha, or, possibly, uncanonical man-lion cults. The image shown in the illustration is an example of this. The main emphasis is upon the lion characteristics of fierceness, bravery and independence that claim almost universal admiration, while the figure of Lakshmi on Vishnu's left knee is a reference to Lakshmi-Narayana figures such as that illustrated on plate 9. The posture, with the legs held in position by a meditation-band (*yoga-patta*), usually belongs to the Girija or Yoga-Narasimha forms. The club, under the lower left hand, is one of Vishnu's attributes and is described in some texts as symbolizing the power of knowledge, and the seven-headed serpent probably represents Shesha on whom he sleeps while creation is suspended. His upper right and left hands hold a wheel and a conch respectively, and his other right hand is in *abhaya mudra*.

14 **Narasimha**, the fourth incarnation of Vishnu as a man-lion; bronze. South India (probably Madras); 19th century.
14.2cm   527 (I.S.)

PLATE 15

Vamana

The first four incarnations, in which Vishnu appears either as an animal, or a half-human half-animal creature, make up a group which is sometimes regarded as appearing during the first (*Krita-*) *yuga* of the *mahayuga* cycle (*see pl.13*). The *avataras* that belong to the following *yugas* are all in human form. The 'first, Vamana, is perhaps significantly a dwarf thus symbolizing the undeveloped state of mankind at the beginning of the second (*Treta-*) *yuga*. As with the legends relating to the first four incarnations, the story behind Vamana is also connected with creation. It concerns Bali, the great-grandson of Hiranyakashipu mentioned in the description of the last plate who was, in contrast, a virtuous and just monarch. His rule was so successful that his reputation began to overshadow that of Indra who was obliged to seek Vishnu's help in order to regain his supremacy. Not wishing to use harsh measures against such an exemplary ruler Vishnu resorted to a stratagem. He disguised himself as a dwarf and asked Bali to give him a piece of land three paces wide on which he could sit and meditate. Pleased to be able to encourage piety Bali granted the request. Vishnu then used his supernatural powers to take possession of heaven and earth in two steps thus depriving Bali of his kingdom. In recognition of Bali's generosity and benevolent rule, Vishnu refrained from taking his third step and gaining the underworld as well but installed Bali as its monarch. The story of Vishnu's three steps (*trivikrama*) and his appearance as a dwarf is a creation myth containing much important symbolism some of which is as old as the *Rig Veda*. The three steps are regarded as holding up elements of the universe; all creatures dwell within them, and their extent symbolizes Vishnu's power to cover the universe.

The image shown in the illustration, in accordance with textual descriptions, holds a water-pot in its right hand and an umbrella in its left, and shows Vamana before his transformation into Vishnu Trivikrama, capable of taking the three enormous strides, images of whom are seldom found in bronze.

15 **Vamana**, the dwarf and fifth incarnation of Vishnu; bronze. South India (probably Madras); 19th century. 15.5cm   692 (I.S.)

PLATE 16

Parashurama

With this incarnation there is a change from the type of mythology on which the preceding *avataras* were based. Most of the stories relating to the other five incarnations, although inconsistent, are on a superhuman plane whereas those about Parashurama usually have a more worldly element and may reflect struggles for economic and political power which took place at an early stage in Indian history. The story behind the name and appearance of this *avatara* concerns a sage's son, Rama, who became a brilliant archer. In gratitude for having this skill conferred on him he went to the Himalayas and did penance to Shiva for many years. Shiva was pleased with this devotion and, when fighting broke out between the gods and demons, ordered Rama to go and defeat the demons. Rama at that time was without his bow and he asked Shiva how he could comply without anything to fight with. Shiva assured him that if he did as he was told he would conquer the demons and this Rama was able to do. As a reward, Shiva gave Rama many gifts and weapons; one of these was a magnificent axe (*parashu*) after which Rama was known as Parashurama ('Rama-with-the-axe'). Vishnu, however, in another story had become his Parashurama incarnation for an entirely different reason. This was the result of a feud which had grown up because a king had stolen his hermit father's wish-granting cow. Parashurama, who had demonstrated his filial piety by beheading his mother at his father's request and then having her brought to life again, took his revenge for the theft by killing the king. In return the king's sons killed Parashurama's father. Vishnu took the form of Parashurama not only to get revenge but to rid the world of all oppression by kings, which he did in the course of 21 battles. Parashurama is the first incarnation in which Vishnu appears in a completely human form while at the same time keeping his status as a deity. His images, as with the other human incarnations, are relatively stable in their iconography. They are almost always two-handed and, similar to the figure in the illustration, hold an axe in their right hand.

16 **Parashurama**, the sixth incarnation of Vishnu; bronze.
South India (probably Madras); 19th century.
15.3cm   528 I.S.

PLATE 17

Rama

From a comparatively minor incarnation whose task was to kill a demon king who held his wife captive, the story of Rama has entered deeply into Indian life as a deity, a subject for literature, and an example of moral excellence. As one of the chief protagonists in Indian epic poetry he has passed into the mythology of countries other than India whose cultures have been influenced by it or its regional variations. In spite of this, his iconography in Indian bronzes is almost entirely restricted to the form shown in the illustration (standing, with two arms one of which holds a bow) although in cases where the bow has been cast separately it is sometimes missing.

This weapon connects him with his brother, the sixth incarnation (*see pl.16*), through the incident in which the Shaivite Parashurama, annoyed by Rama breaking Shiva's bow in a contest, attempted to punish him in a fight. It is likely that the bow, which became Rama's distinguishing attribute, also symbolized masculine virtues through the technique of its use needing a subtle application of strength. It is, however, rather for his qualities of fidelity, gentleness and steadfastness that he has become in Indian society endowed with the ideal qualities of manhood. In the same way his wife Sita is regarded as the embodiment of all that is most admired in Indian womanhood – faithfulness and affectionate compliance. As each was the other's only partner they are also looked upon as setting an example of constancy in marriage. The ways in which these qualities were demonstrated by both Rama and Sita are described in the *Mahabharata* and, at greater length, in the *Ramayana* ('The adventures of Rama') both of which are too long to be summarized here, but are available in English translations.

17 **Rama** or **Ramachandra**, the seventh incarnation of Vishnu; bronze. South India (probably Madras); late 18th or early 19th century. 13.7cm I.M. 16–1909

PLATE 18

Shatrughna and Lakshmana

In the stories about Rama, mentioned in the previous caption, the incidents on which the plot is based and which drive the narrative forward originate in the relationships between him and members of his family, in particular his father, mother, step-mothers and half-brothers. Conventionally, Rama is accorded the status of being the seventh incarnation but, because of the way in which they were conceived, his half-brothers also each inherited part of Vishnu's divinity. Thus the two deities illustrated opposite qualified as objects of worship and became part of the Hindu pantheon. They shared the same father (Dasharatha) as Rama but whereas his mother was Kausalya theirs was Sumitra. Shatrughna holds a fly-whisk (*chamara*) in each hand and Lakshmana a bow (now missing) in a two-armed posture similar to Rama. The image on the right is in an interesting technique, often associated with Tanjore, that combines bronze and brass in the same casting so that the lighter metal is used for details such as the loin-cloth, jewellery, etc.

It will be noticed that these figures (and others illustrated in this booklet) stand with their body flexed at the waist with the weight taken on one leg. This results in a position rather like an S which is shown more clearly in the right-hand figure. It gives much grace to many images in Indian sculpture and suggests that it may be derived from dancing. Indian sculpture recognizes three types of flexion, depending on its degree, and these are called in South India, *abhanga* (slight), *samabhanga* (equal i.e. straight), and *atibhanga* (much). In North India less distinction seems to be made and S-bends are more often described simply as *tribhanga*. Among the images illustrated in this booklet, the one in plate 25 is in *abhanga* posture, plate 32 is in *samabhanga*, and plate 48 in *atibhanga*.

18 **Shatrughna** (*left*), half-brother of Rama; bronze.
South India (probably Madras); 19th century.
14cm   I.M. 61–1914
Lakshmana (*right*), half-brother of Rama; bronze and brass.
South India (probably Tanjore); 19th century.
14.3cm   705 (I.S.)

PLATE 19

Yashoda

This image illustrates an incident of the birth of Krishna, some aspects of which resemble the story of Herod slaying all the children of Bethlehem under two years old (Matt. 2.16) although there is no evidence that there is any direct connexion. Vasudeva, a mythological king, had several wives, including Devaki and Rohini. After Devaki's wedding, her brother (Kamsa) had a premonition that her eighth son would kill him. Dissuaded from killing Devaki immediately, in response to a plea for mercy by Vasudeva, Kamsa proceeded to kill the first six of Devaki's sons. During her seventh pregnancy, Vishnu transferred the embryo to Rohini's womb in order to prevent the child's murder and it was announced that Devaki had miscarried. When the child was born it was called Balarama (see plate 25, where a slightly different story of this incident taken from another text is given). Then Vishnu allowed himself to be conceived in Devaki, and the Goddess of Sleep and Night to be conceived in Yashoda, wife of the cowherd Nanda, both of whom looked after Rohini in their country retreat. But Vishnu was now Devaki's eighth son whom her brother had sworn to destroy. By his power, however, Vishnu had arranged that Devaki and Yashoda should give birth at the same time and that Yashoda would forget the sex of her child. During the night Vasudeva took his son and left him with Yashoda in exchange for her daughter whom he took back to Devaki. Thus Vishnu was born as Krishna and was brought up by Nanda and Yashoda in the safety of the country, and Vasudeva and Devaki could pretend that their eighth child was a daughter. This addition to the Krishna legend, which could be as early as the 4th century A.D., was both the result of the *bhakti* movement (*see pls.8 and 30*) and provided yet more stories for its enrichment.

19 **Yashoda**, holding the child Krishna on her hip; brass. South India; 19th century.
17cm   653 (I.S.)

PLATE 20

Krishna

This incarnation is probably the most important of the ten. It has accumulated a great variety of myths with the result that, as well as being a human incarnation (*see pls.15–18*), Krishna shows all the aspects of human development usually associated with childhood, adolescence, adulthood, etc. There are few stages in a mortal worshipper's life, or objects of his aspiration, for which a counterpart cannot be found somewhere in the stories relating the actitivies of Krishna. It is this almost universal appeal that is responsible for his wide popularity and the deep impression he has made on Indian life. This reputation was only achieved gradually. As with other incarnations he began unobtrusively in the ancient texts but showed an almost organic tendency to develop that was, possibly, only equalled by the rest of the Vishnu legends together. Although many of the stories about him concern his super-human deeds he also revealed a marked human capacity for drinking, fighting and amorous escapades. Most of these are found in the *Mahabharata*, especially in its later interpolation the *Bhagavad-Gita* which is almost entirely devoted to him, and the *Bhagavata-Purana*.

Perhaps the most popular of these stories are about his skill as a flute-player, illustrated by the image opposite which (as is often the case) lacks its flute. This adds considerably to the pastoral character of many of the Krishna stories and, at the same time, its music and shape and the effect it has on the girl cowherds (*gopis*) provide a rich source of speculation on its symbolism (*see also pl.23*). On hearing the music of Krishna's flute, peacocks dance and other animals stand still and worship him with their glances, celestial maidens flying in their aerial cars above the earth become infatuated with him and shower him with flowers, rivers become smooth-running and offer him lotuses, and in the heat of the day clouds let fall on him their cooling rain.

20 **Krishna**, the eighth incarnation of Vishnu, as a flute-player, (*Venugopala*); bronze and brass.
South India (Tanjore); 19th century.
13.4cm I.M. 72–1930.

PLATE 21

Krishna Kaliyadamana

The story that this image illustrates belongs to Krishna's adolescence. It concerns a fight that he had with the snake Kaliya who had previously quarrelled with Garuda (*see pl.29*) whom Kaliya had neglected to honour with the gift of an offering. After being wounded by Garuda, Kaliya took refuge in a pool of water from which Garuda had been excluded because of one of his own previous misdeeds. Besieged in the pool Kaliya poisoned it with his potent venom to such an extent that its vapour was as lethal to birds and animals as its water one drop of which caused instant death. When Krishna heard that his friends the cow-herds, and their flocks, had been poisoned in this way he rushed to their aid, revived them with one ambrosia-like glance, kicked Kaliya almost to death and then danced on him. Kaliya's friends and relatives begged for Krishna's mercy and Kaliya was spared to become one of Krishna's worshippers.

This story is another version of the interminable conflict, in Indian mythology, between Garuda and the *nagas* (*see pl.29*). The bird Garuda symbolizes good, the creation of the world (from the cosmic egg), and salvation, whereas *nagas* often represent evil, death and the underworld. Although Kaliya is reprieved, Garuda and the *nagas* remain enemies and the battle is never resolved. Only Vishnu, who sleeps on the serpent Shesha (*see pl.27*) and uses Garuda as his vehicle, appears to call a truce but this is merely because he is the creator of the universe and thus reconciles all conflicts.

The image opposite holds a ball of butter in its right hand and is therefore similar to another image that has a similar posture but is without the snake, having its right foot resting on a lotus. This is said to be Krishna dancing with the butter ball and it is possible that this image is intended to show two incidents in Krishna's life.

21 **Krishna Kaliyadamana**; bronze.
South India (Tanjore); late 19th century.
17.5cm   I.M. 3–1934

PLATE 22

Krishna as a boy stealing the butter ball

Perhaps some of the most engaging aspects of the Krishna legend are the stories of his boyhood. Although his divinity is never left in doubt, it is subordinated to the more human side of his nature. Thus he is described as a mischievous, rather spoilt, child whose mother was inclined to overlook the pranks he played on her and their neighbours. In the incident shown opposite, he climbed up to where storage jars containing milk, butter, and curds were hung from the ceiling of his house and broke them and played with the butter that fell out. He, and his brother Balarama (*see pl.25*), untied the neighbour's calves and let them run away or chased them and held on to their tails. Worse still, they deliberately used their neighbours' newly-cleaned houses as a toilet in order to annoy them. When they complained to Krishna's mother she was reluctant to be cross with him, as he looked so innocent, and merely smiled at him indulgently.

One day, however, it seemed as if he had gone too far and had been caught eating earth. When he was reproached by his mother he denied that he had done so and invited her to look in his mouth and see for herself. And here the legend finds it necessary to remind us that Krishna is, after all, the supreme god, and tells us that when his mother looked in his mouth she saw not earth but the whole of the universe with its tangible aspects such as the sphere of the earth with its continents, mountains, oceans, lightning, fire and wind, together with all the planets and stars, as well as the intangibles such as the Soul, Time, Nature, Mind and Destiny.

Although some of these pranks are illustrated in paintings few of them form subjects for sculpture. The one illustrated here is probably the most popular and is found in metal sculpture from several parts of India. The basic form is usually the same, with one hand, foot, and knee on the ground and the right hand holding the butter ball, but the variety of the details such as the headdress and jewellery is almost endless. One group that may be identified with some degree of accuracy as coming from South India comprises images with a headdress in the form of an inverted cone as shown opposite.

22 **Krishna as a boy stealing the butter ball**; brass.
South India; late 19th century.
7.5cm   652 (I.S.)

PLATE 23

Krishna and Radha

The captions to plates 8, 46 and 48 refer to the evolution of female deities (*shaktis*), and their function in Hindu worship, which took place mainly between the eighth and twelfth centuries. Between the twelfth and fifteenth centuries another development took place which was unlike anything that had gone before. Krishna and his female partner became associated with ideas of intense romantic love about which many stories, and poems such as the *Gita govinda* of Jayadeva, were written. The reasons for this are obscure as the object of Krishna's emotional fervour, Radha, involved an apparent disregard for Indian social conventions since she was already married. Although marriages at this time were (as often now) a matter of arrangement fidelity was implicit and whereas in the older texts infidelity (including incest) between the gods was commonplace but remote like the gods themselves, the stories of Krishna and Radha were set in everyday circumstances. Moreover, many of the stories about them seemed to place emphasis on female beauty and refer unmistakably to the pleasures of physical love.

The religious content of the Krishna movement is therefore ambiguous; Krishna is a god, but his relationship with Radha both offends and transcends conventional morality. Stories about them have a secular and a religious content, and the levels of symbolism that can be attributed to the details are therefore considerably increased, from the superficial to the complex. The sense in which they can be appreciated is also equally varied depending upon whether they convey deep spiritual insight, or are tales of romantic love or thinly disguised eroticism. Running through all, it is probably their theme of unfulfilled aspiration, represented on the one hand by Radha's love for someone who was not her husband, and on the other by the worshipper's desire for union with his god, that finds a wide interest and largely accounts for their popularity. Illustrations of the Krishna and Radha stories are found more often in painting than sculpture and concern their secular, rather than their religious, appeal. The shrine shown opposite, in contrast, represents their religious aspect as objects of worship.

23 **Krishna and Radha**: brass.
South India; 19th century.
28cm   718 (I.S.)

PLATE 24

The child Krishna lying on a fig leaf

This is an example of one of the less common forms of Indian image in which the deity is shown lying down (for another *see pl.27*). Here, Krishna is said to symbolize God brooding over the ocean of chaos caused by the destruction of the cosmos at the end of an aeon, though the precise nature of the symbolism is unclear.

The cycle of creation and destruction on which much Hindu philosophy is based is mentioned above (*see pls.12 and 13*). Both aspects are often contained in the same image, as here, but in addition the deity can be a witness of the destruction of the cosmos and the cosmos itself. As the Cosmic Man, his hips are formed by the surface of the earth and the dome of the sky is like his deep navel. The myriads of stars form his chest, the other gods his arms, the cardinal points of the compass his ears. Sound is his sense of hearing, fragrance his sense of smell and fire his mouth. The sky is his eyes and the sun his ability to see; day and night are his eyelids, water his palate. The whole of the Vedas are the capacity of his skull, Yama (the god of death) is his incisor teeth, and illusion (*maya*) his laugh. Creation appears again as his sidelong glance. Modesty is his upper lip, greed the lower, the righteous path is his chest (again) and the unrighteous his back. The rivers of the earth are his arteries, trees his hair, and the wind his breath.

This description, from part of the *Bhagavata-Purana*, linking sections of the universe with aspects of the body of God in the form of Krishna, is in contrast with the vision of the cosmos seen in his mouth by his mother as described in the caption to plate 22 above. These, and the ideas of creation and destruction mentioned above, are probably two of the most fundamental aspects of Indian religion and directly or indirectly affect the majority of images shown in this booklet.

24 **The child Krishna lying on a fig leaf** (Krishna Vatapatrashayin); copper and bloodstone. South India (Tanjore); 19th century.
H. 4.8cm L. 11.4cm   I.M. 75–1930

PLATE 25

Balarama

The brothers Krishna and Balarama were sons of Vishnu and are therefore sometimes regarded as joint incarnations. Some sects hold that Krishna is a full incarnation and substitute Balarama for Rama in seventh place.

According to the *Vishnu-Purana* Vishnu took two of his hairs, one black and one white, and implanted them in Devaki's womb. Shortly before their birth they were miraculously transferred to Rohini's womb in order to prevent the infants from being murdered at birth by the tyrant king Kamsa. After they were born it was noticed that Krishna was dark complexioned and Balarama light. They grew up together, shared many adventures, and quarrelled with each other from time to time but Balarama has never become as popular as Krishna.

Both brothers seem to have been the most human of the human incarnations. Neither of them had the aspect of saintliness that can be found in Ramachandra, and both displayed normal human weaknesses even when participating in super-human exploits. In one of these Balarama ordered the river Yamuna to move closer to him so that it would be more convenient to bathe and, when it did not, irritably bullied it into doing what he wanted with his plough. In the *Mahabharata* he is described as a skilful teacher of fighting with the club (*gada*). This weapon, and a plough, are his most usual attributes and he is shown holding them in the illustration opposite.

Deities other than Vishnu appear as incarnations in different forms. In some texts Balarama is described as an incarnation of the serpent king Sheshsa (*see pl.27*) and is therefore an incarnation of two different deities.

25 **Balarama**, sometimes the eighth incarnation of Vishnu; bronze. South India (probably Madras); 19th century.
16cm   594 (I.S.)

PLATE 26

Kalkin

From references in Indian literature there can be little doubt that the horse made a profound impression on ancient India. Although it is likely that the use of horses was already known, there is a strong possibility that new skills in horse breeding and management, and chariot driving, entered India together with other aspects of Aryan culture. The effect appears to have been limited, however, as Indians did not gain a reputation for breeding or the military use of horses as the Arabs and Mongols did later nor did they seem to take to horsemanship as readily as the North American Indians or the Australian aborigines. This is reflected in the association between horses and religion in India which is fitful and sporadic. As the fleetest form of mobile power they were understandably connected with the motion of some gods and thus inevitably with the path of the sun and therefore with sun-gods (see pl.1). Many aspects of solar deities (e.g. Surya and the Ashvins) are to do with horses. In the same way, because only the wealthy could afford to keep horses they became closely linked with kingship, and the *ashvamedha* (horse-sacrifice) bestowed the highest status of supremacy on the rulers who performed it.

As the future incarnation Kalkin will come at the end of the present *Kali-yuga* (see pl.13) when moral excellence no longer exists, the rule of law has disappeared and all is darkness. In some texts he is described as riding a white horse and holding a flaming sword, in some as four-armed holding a sword, conch-shell, wheel and an arrow, and in others as a human having the head of a horse and holding attributes as above but with a club instead of an arrow. The image shown in the illustration seems to have been based on an unidentified text and lacks the arrow or club (the sword, held in the lower left hand, is broken).

26 **Kalkin**, the tenth incarnation of Vishnu as a horse; bronze. South India (probably Madras); 19th century. 9.4cm   592 (I.S.)

PLATE 27

Vishnu reclining on the serpent Shesha

According to Hindu mythology a residue of cosmological substance is left over from the last age of creation from which a new cycle may be brought into existence. This is symbolized by the many-headed serpent-king Shesha, whose name means remainder (sometimes called Ananta, i.e. endless), floating on an ocean which is thought to be like the universe. Vaishnavites believe that during this interval in the cycles of creation Vishnu lies asleep on the coils of Shesha protected by its hoods spread out above his head. There he rests as the source of the Universe until he is ready to begin a fresh cycle. When this has been completed he takes his place in the Vaik-untha heaven as ruler of the world.

Reclining on Shesha, he is said to have a lotus growing out of his navel supporting Brahma (see pls.2 and 3) on its petals as shown in the illustration opposite. In this illustration he also has Lakshmi and Bhudevi (see pl.8) seated at the back and Garuda (see pl.29) kneeling in front.

In another story of the creation, Shesha was used as a rope which, twisted round the world axis resting on a tortoise (see pl.12), the gods pulled back and forth so churning the waters of creation and thus beginning a new cycle.

The illustration opposite shows two of the main forms of headdress (mukuta) found on Indian bronzes. Vishnu wears his characteristic, semi-cylindrical mitre with a flattened knob on top (kiritamukuta fig.I,e), and the goddesses a style associated with female deities having a more conical shape and a more complicated top (karandamukuta fig.I,f). Conventionally, Shiva wears his hair piled in loops on top of his head (jatamukuta fig.I,d) (see pl.31) although sometimes it is almost indistinguishable from the karandamukuta as in plates 32, 33 and 34.

27 **Vishnu**, reclining on the serpent Shesha; bronze. South India (perhaps Tanjore); early 19th century. 8.5cm I.M. 159–1929

PLATE 28

Vitthali

This image is regarded as being a form of Vishnu or Krishna. His name can mean 'standing on a brick' (as opposite), and he is also known as Vithoba or Panduranga. He is usually shown with a headdress similar to the one in the illustration, and standing with his hands on his hips. He is worshipped in particular at Pandharpur, not far from Bombay. Mention has already been made above (pls.6 and 9) to the growth in the number of deities during the development of Hinduism. The reasons for this phenomenon can only be surmised since the accounts of their origin have evidently become mythical. In the case of Vitthali the mythical element is small and, in spite of embellishments, the story may represent the way in which deities often arose. The narrative is basically one of simple folk, in which divine intervention plays a minor part. It tells of a pious brahman, Pundali, who set out with his wife and parents on a pilgrimage to Banaras. During the journey, he paid more attention to the well-being of his wife than to his father and mother. Although this neglect of a son's duties distressed his parents they did not reproach him. On the way they halted at Pandharpur and stayed at the house of another brahman. Pundali was impressed by the contrast between his host's filial care and his own neglect, and began to reflect on its meaning and consequences. One morning he noticed three beautiful female servants and asked them who they were. They told him they were three river-goddesses, Ganga, Yamuna, and Sarasvati but asked him not to approach them as his filial neglect made him a sinner. Crestfallen by this and the resulting inability to cross these three rivers on his journey, Pundali abandoned the pilgrimage and meditated on what had led up to his failure. Consequently he changed his attitude towards his parents and from that time zealously performed his filial duty. This was witnessed by Vishnu who expressed his satisfaction by appearing before Pundali and blessing him. Soon, a special cult of Vishnu, now called Vitthali, grew up at Pandharpur which developed into a sect (the Varkari). Eventually, the prestige of Vitthali grew until Pandharpur became a popular place of pilgrimage.

28 **Vitthali**; gilt bronze. Probably from Pandharpur (Maharashtra); late 18th or 19th century.
15.2cm I.M. 78–1930

PLATE 29

Garuda

Most of the more important Hindu deities are provided with animal, or bird, mounts (*vahanas*) on which they travel about the universe. The origin, and underlying purpose, of these mounts is obscure. It may be linked indirectly with the rural nature of ancient Indian society in which animals were endowed with superhuman powers, or the convention may have been imported from Mesopotamia where deities were sometimes given similiar mounts. Alternatively, *vahanas* may have been regarded as representing essential qualities of the deity in animal form. Although some, or all, of these may be partly the reason for the existence of *vahanas* they fall short of providing a satisfactory explanation.

This is illustrated by the figure of Garuda who is often shown as the mount of Vishnu. He was originally (in the *Rig Veda*) regarded as the sun in the form of a bird but this association was taken over by Surya (*see pl.1*). In Epic literature he is first designated as Vishnu's mount and, in addition, through close family ties, brought into relationship with the tribe of serpents (*nagas, see pl.21*) with whom in later mythology he eventually became involved in almost continuous conflict. By the end of the Gupta period his place as a sun god declined and from about the 9th century onwards he is mainly represented carrying Vishnu on his back or alone, kneeling, and facing the entrance to Vaishnavite temples. His earliest appearance in Indian sculpture was as a mythical bird forming part of the animal kingdom paying homage to the Buddha. The necessity of emphasizing its mythological aspect resulted in characteristic distortions of its form combining, sometimes, a parrot-like beak and human elements and wearing earrings. By the end of the Pallava period the bird element in his appearance has shrunk to a beak-like nose and wings attached to an otherwise human body. In this form he is usually shown with two hands (often in *anjali* pose as opposite) but he may have four when he is supporting Vishnu-Narayana.

29 **Garuda**, the vehicle of Vishnu; bronze.
South India (probably Tanjore); 18th or 19th century.
34.3cm   I.M. 118–1911

PLATE 30

Ramanuja

The results of the first effects of *bhakti* on Indian art have been mentioned in the Introduction (p. vi). Interest in this movement continued, and was followed by another upsurge about the sixth or seventh century which was reflected in an increase in texts such as the later Puranas and Tantras that intensified devotion to a personal god. Thus he was the ultimate reality to whom the devotee directed a passionate and unswerving devotion and service.

Inevitably devotees (*bhaktas*) arose whose piety and learning stood out above the rest. Some of these attracted followers who sought their teaching in the hope of experiencing a more satisfying religious fulfilment. Many of them only acquired local influence, but the fame of others spread to much wider areas particularly in the south. Some of them wrote devotional songs and poetry in their own language, instead of the learned Sanskrit, which strongly appealed to the simple faith of the masses. Eventually some of these sages (*rishis*) were recognized as teachers (*acharyas*), while others achieved near-deification and became 'saints' (*alwars* in Vaishnavite, and *nayanars* in Shaivite, sects).

There is a formal list of 63 Shaiva saints (*see pl.49*) and 12 Vaishnava although others have been added subsequently. This last group includes several historical personages such as the *acharya* Ramanuja who, like his famous predecessor Shankaracharya (A.D. c.850), gave the devotional movement in India a firm philosophical basis. Both of these, as well as the other saints, are sometimes represented as images. Their iconography seems to be somewhat irregular; they are shown seated, or standing, often with their hands in the gesture of prayer (*anjali mudra*) as in the illustration opposite. The object carried in the crook of Ramanuja's left arm, similar to an axe, is said to be a piece of cloth for straining water attached to a staff.

30 **Ramanuja** (d. 1137 A.D.); copper.
South India; late 18th or 19th century.
22.5cm   I.M. 33–1936

PLATE 31

Shiva Somaskanda

One of the two large groups into which Hinduism eventually divided focused its spiritual attention on Vishnu (*see above pl.6*) and the other on Shiva. The division is not entirely clear cut, however, and a tendency towards the fragmentation and assimilation of dogma has never ceased. Broadly speaking, in contrast to Vishnu's reputation as a benevolent creator god, Shiva represents destruction, austerity and the more malignant forces of life. This is an over-simplification and should be seen in the context of creation and destruction being a continuous part of the life cycle. This divergence has the effect that, whereas Vishnu manifested himself through *avataras* (*see pls.11–26*), Shiva is represented by different aspects of his own powers.

Shiva was not a Vedic god but his spiritual ancestor, Rudra, is mentioned in the *Rig Veda*. At this time his character was ambiguous being both benevolent and malevolent, but the latter aspect gradually prevailed. As it became stronger his association with fire remained as part of his function as a destroyer as well as having other symbolic meanings (*see pl.35*). The combination of the ideas of creation and destruction is expressed in his late aspect as the Supreme Being (Mahadeva); in this form he is frequently shown as the phallic symbol (*linga*) in conjunction with the female organ (*yoni*) which are often the point of worship in a Shaivite temple. Some of the characteristics of Shiva, seen on the image opposite, are the formalised knot of matted hair, *jatamukuta*, (symbolizing stored up ascetic power), the crescent moon (*chandra*) on its left (symbol of creation), the third eye the fire from which causes destruction, the axe (upper right hand), and the antelope (upper left hand). He may also hold a small drum (*damaru*) and wear a tiger skin and jewellery in the form of snakes. The lower right hand is in the hand-gesture (*mudra*) symbolizing protection (*abhaya*) and the lower left hand *ahuya-varada*.

The second part of the name of the image illustrated opposite implies that the image originally formed part of a group of three, with his wife Uma and his son Skanda (*see pl.38*).

31 **Shiva Somaskanda**; bronze.
South India; late 18th or early 19th century.
21.3cm I.M. 111–1924

PLATE 32

Shiva Chandrashekhara

The name of this form of Shiva implies that it has the moon (*chandra*) in its headdress but this symbol is not confined to images of Chandrashekhara (*see pl.31*). In the illustration opposite it is on the left (proper) side of the headdress. He has the axe (*parashu*) in his rear right hand and the antelope in his rear left; his front right hand is in the protection hand pose (*abhaya mudra*) and the left in charity (*varada mudra*). He stands in the upright, unflexed *samabhanga* posture (*see pl.18*; for another unflexed image *see pl.50*). He wears earrings (*kundalas*) in the form of the mythical reptile *makara*, snake jewellery, a head (probably intended to be a skull) in his headdress, finger- and toe-rings, and a loin cloth of tiger skin. Other images of Shiva may hold a drum (*damaru*), trident (*trishula*), a noose (*pasha*) etc., etc. according to his form. The ways in which he came to acquire these attributes are described in texts (*see Introduction, p. vii*).

A rather late (about 6th–8th century A.D.) text describes how Shiva acquired some of the ones with which he is often shown; he became involved in a fight with some sages (*rishis*) who sent snakes, a tiger, a lion, and·a demon to back up their curses and efforts to defeat him. But he overcame them all and used them as emblems of his victory. Similarly, the moon (symbolizing his powers of creation and destruction) and the skull (part of a garland of skulls that he wears at the end of the universe) are accounted for. The image of Chandrashekhara also exemplifies the way in which, in Hindu iconography, deities proliferate. He has two other forms; one in which he is identical with the one opposite but is accompanied by his wife Uma, and another where they are together but he has his left arm round her left shoulder.

32 **Shiva Chandrashekhara**, bronze.
South India; 18th or 19th century.
44.8cm   I.M. 36–1937

PLATE 33

Virabhadra

This deity is a form of Shiva who created him to act as his henchman in his quarrel with Daksha. There are several versions of this antagonism in texts such as the *Kurma- Varaha-*, and *Bhagavata-Puranas*, as well as several others some of which link Virabhadra with Vishnu. In this group Virabhadra holds a sword and shield in his two front hands, and an arrow (*left*) and bow in his two back hands; he has a garland of skulls, wears sandals and has a fierce expression on his face. On his right with hands in *anjali mudra* stands Daksha, a complex deity who first appears in the *Rig Veda*. As with many Indian deities Daksha's function changed from time to time, but one of them was connected with an interpretation of his name as 'skilful in ritual'. It is this aspect of his character which is related to the group shown in the illustration opposite. The story describes how Daksha, who was excitable and aggressive, offended Shiva by not inviting him to attend a sacrifice that Daksha had arranged to perform. Shiva's wife Sati (one of Daksha's daughters, *right*) wanted to attend the sacrifice but Shiva told her of the enmity between him and Daksha and advised her not to go. However, she ignored her father's wish and went to Daksha's house to witness the ceremony. While she was there Daksha so grossly insulted her husband (Shiva) and humiliated her, that she committed suicide by jumping into the pit containing the sacrificial fire. Enraged by this Shiva created Virabhadra as a form of himself, gave him an army, and sent him to punish Daksha which he did successfully by cutting off Daksha's head in the battle. The other gods, fearing that the loss of Daksha's pre-eminence in ritual procedure might interfere with the effectiveness of their own sacrifices, begged Shiva to bring him back to life. Shiva agreed but, as Daksha's head could not be found, Brahma substituted the head of the goat that had been cut off in the ritual sacrifice.

33 **Virabhadra**, brass.
South India (Madras); 19th century.
22cm   880 (I.S.)

PLATE 34

Shiva and Parvati (Uma Maheshvara)

It is instructive to compare this illustration with the image of Vishnu and Lakshmi shown on plate 9 which has almost the same iconography except for the symbols held by the two male deities (here an axe and an antelope). In some respects the two female deities are also related; Vishnu's Lakshmi in her form as Sita, and Shiva's Parvati in her form as Sati (see pl.33) both represent chastity and virtuousness. Despite this similarity, Lakshmi's character is closer to that of a submissive wife than Parvati's, which she demonstrated by changing her form whenever Vishnu changed his. This did not prevent her from cursing Vishnu on one occasion that his head would drop off, and on another being fickle and wayward.

In contrast to these rather human traits, Parvati's qualities are of a somewhat different order. As Kali (Black) she became an ascetic (see pl.49) whose severe penances were intended to attract the attentions of Shiva. Later, because Shiva teased her about her black skin, she shed it; subsequently it was entered by the combined brilliance of the gods and sages to make Katyayani, another of her forms. All the chief gods gave her weapons and other presents and, in this form (under different names), she fought Mahisha (see pl.47) and other demons.

These two also illustrate the general development of female deities particularly between the fifth and the thirteenth centuries. From being merely the consort of male deities and their active partners, *shaktis* gradually became independent and objects of worship in their own right (see pl.46). Moreover, they no longer helped the gods to carry out their plans but used the gods to achieve success for their own higher purposes. Originally, these were often concerned with the eternal quarrels that arose between the gods and enemies of religion (*asuras*, demons). This slowly changed as the cult of magic and elaborate ritual, which had always been part of folk-religion, began to affect both Buddhism and Hinduism. As a result of Tantrism, as this movement was called, greater emphasis was placed on the destructive element of female deities and their part in interceding on the worshipper's behalf against the forces of evil, or helping with the acquisition of supernatural powers.

Another consequence was that the Energy aspect of *shaktis* was more often seen as the energy of destruction.

34 **Shiva and Parvati** (Uma Maheshvara); bronze.
South India; 19th century.
13.6cm I.M. 62–1914

PLATE 35

Shiva Nataraja

This is a popular image of Shiva, examples of which have been made in bronze from as early as the eleventh century. It illustrates a legend in which Shiva, accompanied by Vishnu disguised as a beautiful woman, set out to subdue ten thousand heretical holy men who were living in a nearby forest. The holy men became angry and evoked a fierce tiger out of a sacrificial fire and sent it against Shiva to kill him. But Shiva merely flayed it and wore the skin as a cape. Next he was attacked by a poisonous snake, but Shiva tamed it and hung it round his neck like a garland. Then the hermits employed a fierce black dwarf to destroy him with a club, but Shiva put one foot on his back and performed a magical dance which was so brilliant that the dwarf and then the holy men acknowledged Shiva as their master.

The symbolism of this dance can be interpreted in different ways. It may represent Shiva as the moving force of the universe and his five supernatural acts of creation, preservation, destruction, embodiment, and release (of the souls of men from illusion). The last purpose might be linked to the idea that release can be found in the fire of the cremation ground, perhaps here symbolized by the ring of flames round the dancer.

Here the figure of Shiva is caught in mid-dance with one foot on the demon and the other poised for the next step; his long hair flies out at the sides, he holds the hour-glass shaped drum, representing the five rhythms of manifestation (*see above*), and the ashes of the fire with which he destroyed the universe.

35 **Shiva Nataraja** ('Shiva as Lord of the Dance'), bronze.
South India (Tanjore); 19th century.
19.3cm   I.M. 71–1930

PLATE 36

Nandin

This animal corresponds with Vishnu's Garuda (*see pl.29*) and other, similar vehicles (*vahanas*). Originally, under the name Nandikeshvara, it seems to have existed in human form as a *rishi* (sage) who belonged to Shiva's retinue, sometimes acting as his door-keeper. There are several accounts in the Puranas of the way in which he achieved divine or semi-divine status. These include his recognition as another form of Shiva from whom, in some cases, his representations are sometimes almost indistinguishable. In this form he may be found at the entrance to Shiva temples but, perhaps more often, he is in the form of a bull similar to the one shown here.

The reasons for the association, which does not at first seem to be relevant, stems from Shiva's relationship with Rudra (*see pl.31*) who was sometimes referred to as a bull. This is likely to have its roots in the vast amount of mythology and symbolism surrounding bulls that is found in ancient cultures, including those of Egypt and Greece, which have contributed to the civilizations of western Asia and Europe. The almost universal attributes of strength and virility are not difficult to identify with some aspects of Shiva, and his link with bulls can be traced to Epic literature (*Mahabharata*) and coinage dating from about the 1st century B.C. – 1st century A.D. In other accounts, the bull was given to Shiva (by Prajapati, The Lord of Progeny), or he took the form of a bull to represent Dharma and stand for the redemption of departed souls on the other side of death.

His association with fertility is illustrated by the custom of touching his testicles when worshippers enter a Shiva temple intending to offer prayers for an increase in the size of their family.

When Nandin is painted he is shown as pure white with a well rounded body, large brown eyes, heavy shoulders, shining coat and black tail. The hump should be like the top of a snow-capped mountain; he should have a golden girth round his body and sharp horns with red points.

36 **Nandin**, the bull vehicle of Shiva; brass.
South India; late 18th or early 19th century.
H. 15.2cm L. 13cm   2162–1883 (I.S.)

PLATE 37

Ganesha

The names of this deity, also called Ganapati, describe him as 'Lord of Hosts' and 'The Remover of Obstacles'. Although he has been identified with deities mentioned in the *Rig Veda* his development into his present form took place much later in some recensions of the *Mahabharata*. Here, and in later texts, there are several accounts of his birth. In one, Parvati (*see pls.38 and 39*) created him from the scurf of her body so that he could act as her door-guardian. When he refused to admit Shiva (*see pls.31 and 32*) the god cut off his head. As Parvati was distressed about this Shiva offered to replace it with the head of the first living being that came along, which happened to be an elephant. According to the *Brihaddharma-Purana*, however, he was conjured out of a piece of cloth by Shiva to make a son for Parvati. Later Shiva brought about the boy's death by decapitation and then, in order to placate Parvati, he called on the gods to find him a new head. After much searching they gave him an elephant's head which had had a tusk broken when it was cut from the body.

Other aspects of his appearance have their explanation in symbolism; his obesity contains the whole universe, his trunk is bent to remove obstacles, and his four arms represent the four categories into which things (e.g. castes, Vedas) can be divided. His companion animal (*vahana*) is a bandicoot. This illustrates the different ways in which obstacles can be removed to reach religious ends; the elephant tramples down everything in its path, but the bandicoot can creep through small holes and cracks to achieve the same goal. When painted he is red in colour but in some texts he is described as yellow. Four arms are the usual number but there may be more as in the case of Maha-Ganapati who has ten, rides on his bandicoot and has a goddess (Siddhi or Buddhi?) on his knee. Other images of him may ride on a lion.

As The Remover of Obstacles he is frequently propitiated by worshippers suffering from an almost unlimited range of calamities, and also at the start of a ritual or beginning of a journey. As a god of wisdom he is invoked by seekers of knowledge. Endowed with a gentle and affectionate nature, he is extremely popular and his images are found in many Shaivite households and acting as a guardian deity on the outskirts of villages.

37 **Ganesha** the elephant-headed god; bronze.
South India; late 18th or 19th century.
15.7cm   I.M. 76–1914

PLATE 38

Skanda

This image probably formed part of a Somaskanda group (*see pl.31*) standing between Shiva and Parvati (or Uma as she is sometimes called). Such groups are relatively common in South Indian sculpture and enable this image to be identified.

The figure, holding a lotus bud in each hand, represents one of the sons of Shiva (*see also pl.37*) as a child. His conception and birth (*see also pl.39*), of which there are several versions, were part of the endless rivalry and war between the deities and demons, which form such a large part of Indian mythology. Their descriptions, such as those found in the *Shiva-Purana*, also illustrate the manifest eroticism which runs through many of these stories.

The world of the gods had become intolerable because of the almost continuous love-play between Shiva and Parvati and the vigour with which it was carried out. The gods asked Shiva to stop, and he agreed but asked them what was to be done with all the semen that had been discharged. They told him to put it on the earth, and afterwards it was taken up by Agni and consumed. Later, Agni regretted what he had done as he felt that it reduced his own powers, but he was afraid to throw it away as its fire might then burn the whole world. He therefore asked the Ganges to accept it as her waters would curb its fire. She agreed, but it eventually became a burden to her as well and she went to Brahma to ask him to help her find relief. When she told him the origin of the semen he told her to go to the mountain of the rising sun and put it on to a pile of special grass. After 10,000 years the semen became the infant Skanda.

38 **Skanda**, bronze.
South India; 18th or 19th century:
20.7cm   1065–1873

PLATE 39

Karttikeya

This deity, who is particularly popular in South India, is also known as Skanda (*see pl.38*) and Subrahmanya as well as by several other names. In some texts (e.g. the *Ramayana*) he is regarded as the son of Shiva and Parvati and is therefore the brother of Ganesha (*see pl.37*). The same text gives another account of his birth and yet other texts give different ones.

Although of relatively recent origin, compared with some Hindu gods, there seems to be evidence that he was in worship during the early centuries A.D., and that his origin might have resulted from the assimilation of a Dravidian deity.

Karttikeya may have one head and two arms, as well as other combinations, but probably his most common form, illustrated opposite, has six heads and twelve arms when he is known as Shadanana-Subrahmanya. The reason for his six heads can be found in one of the stories regarding his birth mentioned above. A passage in the *Mahabharata* describes Agni's adulterous relationship with six wives of the Rishis, who represent the six stars that form the Indian Pleiades in the constellation of Taurus (*see pl.50*), that resulted in the birth of Karttikeya. His six heads enabled them to suckle him and their name, Krittikas, was applied to Skanda as Karttikeya, Son of the Pleiades. He rides on his peacock *vahana* and on each side stands one of his two wives, Devasena (*left proper*), and Valli (*right*). In his hands he holds a *shakti* (kind of spear), arrow, sword, discus, noose, cock, bow, shield, conch and plough, with one hand in *varada-* and the other in *abhaya-mudra*.

In some texts he is described as an army commander or endowed with great strength and skill at arms. He is thus sometimes regarded as a god of war or, as in many Shaivite temples, as a guardian deity.

39 **Karttikeya**, bronze.
South India (Madras); 19th century.
26cm   I.M. 20–1938

PLATE 40

Narada

This is a popular deity, chiefly because he appears in so many Purana stories as a teacher, story-teller, messenger, and sage. In most of them he plays only a minor part but in a few others, such as the one in which he inspires Valmiki to write the *Ramayana*, his role (though small) has a crucial bearing on the outcome. He is alleged to be the author of several hymns in the *Rig Veda* and referred to as a *pandit* in the *Atharva-Veda Samhita*. In another, later, text he is included in a list of 22 incarnations of Vishnu (*see pl.*6); he is sometimes cursed as an eternal wanderer, and at others as a profligate servant of women. There are several versions of his birth; as the son of Kashyapa and one of the daughters of Daksha (*Mahabharata*); born from Brahma's forehead, or his throat; son of Vishvamitra, etc. He appears in some of the Krishna legends, and is credited with the invention of the *vina* by which he is connected with the heavenly musicians (*gandharvas*) of whom he is regarded as the leader. Evidently this reputation made him conceited and Vishnu decided to chasten him. He showed Narada several women with badly cut and bleeding limbs. When Narada asked who they were Vishnu told him that they were Raginis (deified forms of musical modes) who had been injured by his incompetent singing.

As with other deities, he also has a less appealing side to his character. This is illustrated by two of his epithets, 'strife-maker' (Kali-karaka) and 'vile' (Pishuna). All these, and other, references may not have originally been intended for the same person and the possibility remains that they were drawn gradually together by later writers.

It might be expected that a deity, although a relatively minor one, with so many aspects to his birth, life, and character might give rise to many iconographic forms. He is, however, usually shown as a standing figure holding a *vina*, sometimes (as opposite) clean shaven but perhaps more often as a venerable, bearded figure.

40 **Narada**, brass.
South India (Madras); probably first half of 19th century.
27cm   I.M. 128–1924

PLATE 41

Khandoba and Mhalsa

This deity, also called Makhari, Mallari, Martand, etc., is a form of Shiva and is popular in western India where there is a pilgrim shrine erected to him at Jejuri, near Poona, not far from Pandharpur (*see pl.28*). His usual attributes are a sword, trident, drum, and bowl; his vehicle (*vahana*) is a horse, and he may be shown associated with a dog.

The cult of Khandoba is unlikely to be old; the first record of the Jejuri temple belongs to the late fourteenth century which may be later than the beginning of the cult itself. There are at least two stories relating to the early appearance of Khandoba. In one, he made himself known to a number of cowherds who were resting in a field but went away again when one of his most devout worshippers approached. This caused the worshipper acute disappointment, and led to a controversy among the village elders over the significance of a *linga* that was found on the spot where Khandoba appeared. To silence disbelief, a strange contest was held involving cutting lines in the earth. The devout worshipper won, and a shrine to Kandhoba erected at the place where he appeared.

This tale has all the elements of a rustic myth intended to impress villagers, and includes other passages making use of historical material about disputes between prominent local families. The other story is far more sophisticated and links Khandoba more directly to Shiva and even makes reference to Vishnu. It is similar to many others (e.g. about Nataraja, *pl.35* and Mahishasuramardini, *pl.47*), and concerns the intervention of a deity (Shiva) against the ravages wrought by demons against the worlds of gods and men. It includes the reincarnation of two of the demon kings after they had been killed in a skirmish, the inclusion of Vishnu as one of the allies who opposed them, a violent battle on heroic scale, and ultimately Shiva taking the form of Martand (Khandoba) in order to lead the victorious armies. The battle took place on Jayadri mountain, now Jejuri. By association of ideas, Khandoba's wife Mhalsa is assumed to be a form of Parvati although there seems to be little evidence to support this.

41 **Khandoba and Mhalsa**, brass.
Western India; probably first half of 19th century.
21.5cm   I.M. 66&A–1914

PLATE 42

Bhairava

Bhairava is an aspect of Shiva who is often, as here, shown nude, with a third eye, long teeth and hair of flames. He is sometimes given jewellery of snakes, and a garland of skulls which is here stylized into a garland of flowers. In the illustration opposite he has four arms holding (*left*) a snake (*naga*) and trident (*trishula*) (*right*) a noose (*pasha*) and cup (*kapala*), and stands with his dog vehicle (*vahana*) behind him.

There are several other forms of this deity, some having up to five heads and ten arms. In many ways he is similar to the Buddhist Mahakala some forms of which also carry a noose. Both represent a guardian function, in the case of Bhairava as a door guardian (*dvarapala*), when he is also known as Kshetrapala, and of Mahakala as a faith guardian (*dharmapala*). The coincidence is probably not entirely accidental. Both figures appear late in the development of Indian iconography and arose during the period when Tantrism had begun to affect both religions, particularly the cult of Shiva. This was partly an intensification of very old practices such as the use of hand-gestures (*mudras*), and magic (including magic syllables, *mantras*), and the worship of female deities (*shaktis, see pls.8 and 48*) for the purpose of acquiring supernatural powers. These were taught partly through written texts (Tantras), and partly by instruction from a teacher (*guru*) who interpreted the essentially secret rituals described in the texts and without whom they could not be fully comprehended.

One result of the worship of female deities was the development of a group of 64 female ascetics (*yoginis*) who, corresponding to the trend in Indian iconography mentioned elsewhere in these pages (*pls.6 and 34*), acquired a male consort which the texts describe as Bhairavas; but there is little evidence to suggest that their cult was very widespread or more important than the worship of other *yoginis*.

42 **Bhairava**, brass.
South India; 19th century.
8cm   I.M. 64–1914

PLATE 43

Hanuman

Hanuman is a popular deity who is worshipped all over India, particularly in villages and in the South. His story is found in the *Ramayana* where he is the ubiquitous servant, the epitome of devoted service and loyalty. His search for the heroine Sita, captured by Ravana, (*see pl.44*), illustrates his superhuman powers and zealous performance of the tasks that were given to him. Confident of his ability to find her he set off with his retinue of monkey followers to search the southern quarter of the world. At first they were unsuccessful, but eventually heard that she was captive in Lanka (perhaps Shri Lanka). By a prodigious leap he crossed the channel between India and Lanka and, magically changing his form several times, entered the formidable city in which he thought she was imprisoned. After avoiding many guards, and making a number of fruitless attempts at finding her, he eventually discovered that she was confined in a nearby forest. Before releasing her Hanuman attempted to punish Ravana for abducting Sita. Hanuman was captured and his tail set on fire, but, by his divine powers, he escaped and used his tail to burn Lanka to the ground. He returned to Rama without Sita, and helped him in many miraculous ways to besiege Lanka; twice he flew to the Himalayas to collect healing grass and herbs for his wounded companions in the monkey army, and for Lakshmana; finally after the siege was over he was sent to Sita and begged her to return to Rama. After they had been reunited it was time for Hanuman and his monkey army to return to their forest home, but his wish to remain as Rama's faithful servant was granted.

His image is found in many forms, often with one head and two arms, standing in three-quarter, or side, view with a long tail looped over his head. Alternatively, he may stand with two hands held together in *anjali mudra* (as opposite) in front of him. There are several other forms including one with ten arms and five heads – as well as his own, that of a Garuda, boar, horse, and (man-) lion, representing the five most important incarnations of Vishnu.

43 **Hanuman**, the monkey god; brass.
South India; 19th century.
31cm 507 (I.S.)

PLATE 44

Ravana

This image is more often found in painting than in sculpture. In both he frequently has, as here, ten heads and 20 arms (two holding a bow and arrow), but he may have one head and two arms, or carry other weapons and symbols.

He has already been mentioned in the description of the previous plate as the king of Lanka but he was also chief of the demons (*rakshasas*) in human form. Although included in the *Mahabharata*, his main story is found in the *Ramayana* where his fight to defend his kingdom forms one of the most colourful passages. He is described as an experienced warrior who carries wounds on his body from many battles with the gods; he is an expert magician (able, for example, to change his form), belligerent, self-seeking and a bully but carrying out his mischief with a certain amount of style and even occasional acts of chivalry.

In revenge for Rama (*see pl.17*) and Lakshmana defending themselves by killing some of his demon retainers, Ravana kidnapped Rama's wife Sita and carried her off to Lanka in his aerial car. The great battle took place when Rama's armies, helped by Hanuman, went to rescue her. After several unsuccessful attempts Ravana overcame Hanuman by paralysing him with a magic weapon but he managed to escape. This incensed Ravana so much that his anger grew to an even higher pitch and, swearing that he would not be thwarted again, he called a council of his generals. They supported Ravana's plan for vigorous attack on Rama's army, but Ravana's younger brother advised caution and subterfuge. When his word was ignored he deserted to the other side. Ravana, heedless of his brother's counsel and blind to everything but the joy of destruction, flung his army into the fight. The text vividly describes the battle, how on one side hundreds and thousands of monkeys roaring and biting and accompanied by drums tore up trees and used stones as weapons; how, on the other side, the demons (*rakshasas*) replied with clouds of arrows and blows with axes and clubs. Both armies made the air vibrate with the noise of battle and the ground run with the blood of the dead and wounded. At last Rama fought Ravana in single combat; almost defeated by Ravana's hydra-like heads, which grew as soon as they were severed, he finally used his own magic weapon and Ravana fell dead.

44 **Ravana**, Brass.
South India; 19th century.
16cm   729M–1877

PLATE 45

Arjuna and Bhima

These two figures are of characters in the *Mahabharata*, one of the great Indian Epics that are mentioned elsewhere in these pages (*see pls.3,6 and 11*). They are princes of the Pandu family who, with their three brothers, form the protagonists in the drama together with their opponents, the hundred sons of Dhritarashtra, in a struggle for the throne of the Kurus. For much of the story the Pandu princes are either soldiers of fortune or fighting for the family cause. When they are shown as images it is natural that their martial prowess should be indicated as well as their royal status. Thus both brothers here have the headdress, (crown, *kiritamukuta*), jewellery, waistcloth, and pattens of princes, and weapons to illustrate their skill in arms.

Arjuna's most characteristic weapon is probably a bow which he received from Agni, the god of fire, but in the illustration opposite he is given instead a sword and shield. Although not the eldest of the five Pandu princes, Arjuna perhaps came closest to being the ideal son. His father was a god (Indra in his case), he was brave in battle, generous in victory, a staunch friend, upright in his dealings, and handsome in appearance.

Bhima (also called Bhimasena), son of the wind god Vayu, was also a brave warrior whose favourite weapon was the club with which he is shown here. Unlike his brother, however, he lacked a balanced outlook and enjoyed fighting for its own sake. He engaged in several personal combats (some of them marked by great cruelty) in addition to participating zealously in the battles between armies which occur many times in the Epic story. He was a bad-tempered glutton of immense size and strength whose lack of compassion denied him the title hero which his brother Arjuna assumed so readily. At the same time, his exploits undoubtedly add a piquancy and zest to the story and provide a foil against which his brother's rectitude is enhanced.

45 **Arjuna** (*left*) **and Bhima** (*right*), bronze.
South India; 19th century.
left 19.6cm   I.M. 132–1924
right 19.5cm   I.M. 131–1924

PLATE 46

Durga

The deity has eight arms, and holds on the left trident, sword, snake and bell, and on the right, drum, shield, cup and water pot; she is seated in *sukhasana* posture on a double lotus throne and wears a garland of skulls. The *torana* at the back is similar to those shown on plates 10 and 33 with the addition of the conch shell (*right*) and wheel (*left*) symbols usually associated with Vishnu and often held by Durga. Just visible below her left knee, next to the lotus throne is the figure of a lion, (sometimes the mount of Durga).

Durga is a female deity whose relation with her closest male deity (Shiva) is sufficiently remote for her to be worshipped in her own right. It is likely that, not long after female deities appeared as *shaktis* of male deities (*see pls.4 and 8*), goddesses were elevated to the status of independent deities. It is not known which of them, in the earlier stages of this development, first achieved the further distinction of having a temple in which they were the main icon that would give undoubted evidence of final emancipation. This may have taken place about the 7th or 8th century A.D. as the *shakti* of the Impersonal Absolute is referred to as Durga in the *Narayana Upanishad* and as being susceptible to worship for the acquisition of material gain in this world and spiritual advancement in the next, thus suggesting that she was at least semi-independent.

Once female deities became fully independent they responded to the usual forces in Indian religion to take on different forms, as, for example, Devi had already done. As a result they were made vehicles for the assimilation of non-Hindu mythology and practices in the same way as their male counterparts (*see pls.6 and 42*). As well as supplicating a goddess for the bestowal of favours she was invoked for her active and sometime violent assistance against demons, terrors and disasters in the same way that the old gods had used female divinities as their agents in similar struggles. This contributed to the development of a group of fierce-looking female deities in contrast to peaceful ones. Thus in the *Mahabharata* a *shakti* is described as a fierce, black goddess and, in the Upanishad mentioned above, Durga is called a flaming goddess.

46 **Durga**, brass
South India; 19th century.
20.5cm   I.M. 71–1914

PLATE 47

Mahishasuramardini

This is one of the Durga forms of Devi (*see pls.8 and 48*) of whom Mahishasuramardini is one of the earliest variations. By the 4th century A.D., examples are found with two or twelve arms but without her lion mount. Later she is shown either with, or seated on, the animal and her battle with the demon more vividly portrayed.

Descriptions of this deity, given in the *Devimahatmya* section of the *Markandeya-purana*, which may be as early as the 6th or 7th century A.D., vary according to the number of her arms. The two most frequent numbers are ten or, as in the image opposite, eight where she is holding (*left*) trident (missing), sword, arrow, and lotus, (*right*) discus, bow, shield, and the demon's head.

All forms of the deity are based on the story in which the gods were threatened by the demon Mahisha who took the form of a buffalo. Unable to defeat it themselves they went to the Goddess for assistance. She agreed to help but while she was practising austerities in her hermitage it was invaded by the buffalo demon and his army. He made advances towards the Goddess, and when she contemptuously repulsed him he flew into a rage and tried to kill her. The gods came to her assistance by giving her all their weapons to use against him (hence the large number of arms on some of her images). Although the Goddess mounted her lion and trounced the demon's army he returned to the attack on his own, still in his buffalo form. As each struggled to overcome the other, the demon changed his form several more times into a lion, elephant, etc., to try and gain the advantage. At last, with the help of draughts of honeyed wine, she summoned up all her might as the demon returned to his buffalo form and attacked again. But the Goddess pinned him down with her foot on his neck and her trident and then, seizing his sword from his hand, she cut off his head just as he was emerging from the buffalo's mouth and thus finally destroyed him.

47 **Mahishasuramardini**, brass.
South India; 19th century.
19.2cm   729–1877

PLATE 48

Pidari

This image, also known as Pitali, is probably more often found in South India than in the North. She is regarded as being a consort of Shiva through being an aspect of Kali and is described as such in at least one text. Here she holds a noose (?), trident, skull-cup and drum; the last named is entwined by a snake, which is a South Indian characteristic frequently associated with the drum held by Shiva. She has flaming hair, two or three eyes, and in some cases the cup may be rectangular. She may have snakes decorating her breasts, be shown seated, or carry an elephant goad (*ankusha*), instead of a noose. Her fearsome appearance (here indicated merely by long incisor teeth) is intended to frighten off evil spirits against which she is invoked. Although she is sometimes reduced to the status of village deity (*gramadevata*) her history can be traced to inscriptions of the Chola period (about A.D. 850–1279) which refer to her by at least six different names, including Kala-Pidari (i.e. Kali). This illustrates the combined effect of the tendency towards the proliferation of deities (already mentioned several times in these pages), and the emancipation of female deities. It resulted in the development of very many independent goddesses that took place through the influence of Tantrism. This cult, which affected both Buddhism and Hinduism, was popular in several places in India at different times, but reached its peak during the Pala period in Eastern India (about A.D. 750–1162). It has some claims to being an independent sect within which *shakti* worship achieved its own degree of independence. In order to express the ideas which each new *shakti* represented, symbolism became more complex. This affected the colour of the deities, their posture, and the attributes either worn or held in their hands (which became greater in number). These included, as well as the more traditional objects such as swords, tridents, etc., skull-cups (as shown in the illustration opposite), severed heads, and garlands of skulls (*see pl.46*). More emphasis was placed on two aspects of the deities, their fierce appearance and sexual symbolism. The latter (*see pl.34*) reflected a fundamental implication of *shakti* worship represented by the *yoni-linga* symbols of the Shiva cult. It may be partly due to this association that many later female deities are regarded as *shaktis* of Shiva.

48 **Pidari**, bronze
South India; 19th century.
16.4cm   I.S. 46–1980

PLATE 49

Karaikkal-Ammaiyar

Reference has already been made to Vaishnava poet-saints (*alwars*) in the caption to plate 30. In addition to these there is a number of Shaiva and Vaishnava teachers (*acharyas*) who may also be regarded as saints by their followers. These *nayanars* sometimes included women, one of whom is illustrated opposite. She is usually shown, as here, as an emaciated figure but she may also be shown as normal; in each case she often carries a pair of cymbals.

Evidently Karaikkal-Ammaiyar's reputation was partly achieved through her practice of asceticism (*tapas*). This was widespread and had a long history in India, as is shown by incidents in the stories of many deities who subjected themselves to severe austerities and penance. In Indian religious practice asceticism can be divided into two parts, one an extension of the other, but in each the objective is the same – to improve one's ability to achieve one's aim whether it be spiritual or intellectual. It was, and still is, widely believed that by reducing one's dependence on material things, including food and water, to the minimum required to maintain life one's mental faculties could be raised to a supranormal level. This is the first, passive, aspect of asceticism in which merely renunciation plays the most important part. As a result of systematic non-possessing, nature no longer hides her secrets, the wise are content, and all precious (i.e. spiritual) things are acquired, etc., etc. It is a short step to the second, active, application of renunciation which implies the participation in activities that are to some extent painful, difficult, or unnatural and lead to the almost divine powers said to have been acquired by *rishis*.

These powers are mentioned in the earliest Hindu scriptures where those of Brahma sustain the world and those of Indra gain him heaven. Eventually *tapas* became part of Tantrism where it was used in order to try and achieve supernatural powers (*siddhi*). Because of the possibility of its abuse asceticism was rejected by several sects, including Buddhism and Jainism, and by more recent religious teachers.

49 The Shaiva saint **Karaikkal-Ammaiyar**; copper.
South India; 18th or 19th century.
25cm I.M. 118–1924

PLATE 50

Shani (the planet Saturn)

Astrology, for centuries regarded as identical with astronomy, has a legendary origin in India where its main purpose was for ascertaining the correct dates and times for performing sacrifices. It is possible that some early Indian astrological ideas came from Mesopotamia but this is less certain than the evidence of Greek influence. A 3rd century A.D. text, which may be based on a much earlier version, includes Greek astronomical ideas. These were probably transmitted via Alexandria and, by the 6th century A.D., Indian authors clearly attribute much of their information to Hellenistic scientific sources. This is shown by many of the Sanskrit words for planets and signs of the Zodiac that were borrowed from the Greek or Latin such as *leya* (Leo), *ara* (Ares), and *kroda* (Kronos, an equivalent name for Saturn).

But the exchange of ideas was not all one way, and it is likely that from about the eighth century India's own contributions to the science of astronomy were passed to the west either directly by travelling astronomers and mathematicians or through the Arabs. By this time astronomy had established for itself a separate identity which was further strengthened by contacts with the great Muslim universities introduced by the Mughals. Later, with the Sun (Surya, *see pl.1*) and Moon (Soma), India included the five conventional planets, Mercury (Budha), Venus (Shukra), Mars (Mangala), Jupiter (Brihaspati) and Saturn (Shani); the Moon was given two additional aspects, Rahu (its ascending node) and Ketu (its decending node), which were regarded as planets and brought the total to nine. All are represented as images although their iconography (except for Surya) varies considerably.

Shani is often regarded as a bringer of bad luck, and is therefore frequently propitiated. He is described in some texts as holding a staff in one hand, having the other in the gift-bestowing gesture (*varada mudra*), and sitting on a lotus seat, while another text says he should hold a staff and a rosary and ride in a chariot. The identification of the image opposite rests on a similar image in a planet group in a South Indian temple.

Rahu is primarily known as a demonic planet who periodically devours the moon, causing eclipses (or waning). He is often shown as a disembodied head because he stole the Soma (i.e. the moon, where Soma is kept) and drank it. Vishnu saw him do it and beheaded him but, because the Soma had already passed through his head and throat, his head became immortal. Thus in sculpted panels showing the planets Rahu is represented by a head, and a pair of hands since they too touched the Soma.

50 **Shani** (the planet Saturn); bronze.
South India; 19th century.
20.3cm   M.1670

Roman numerals = Introduction
Arabic numerals = Plate nos.